"This is a must-have companion to the CPRT book. Like the book, this is a true second edition, not only updated, but vastly expanded to work with new populations. This manual provides four new *Therapist Protocols* and accompanying *Parent Notebooks*. Experts with each population provide all resources needed to expand working with younger and older children, adoptive families, and teachers. Given the profound research support for CPRT, this new edition provides the filial/CPRT therapist with the tools to forever impact families and classrooms!"

—**Linda E. Homeyer, PhD, LPC-S, RPT-S**, distinguished professor emerita, Texas State University and director emerita, Association for Play Therapy

"The expanded CPRT manual provides child therapists with detailed curriculum to understand and actively use play therapy concepts and skills to improve child-parent relationships and children's emotional and behavioral areas of concern. Bratton and Landreth offer a clear, understandable treatment plan to address the complexity of child-parent relationships, along with providing demonstrable steps to applying the approach. Four new protocols address the unique needs of parents of toddlers and preadolescents, adoptive families, and systemic partners. Child therapists will find this manual to be a valuable tool in their work with parents."

Dee C. Ray, PhD, LPC-S, NCC, RPT-S, distinguished teaching professor and director of the Center for Play Therapy, University of North Texas

"CPRT has been empirically demonstrated to improve child-parent relationships and child behaviors. The expanded treatment manual provides the essentials needed for therapists to implement the program successfully with parents of toddlers through preadolescents and other special populations. The notebook for parents expands on the principles, allowing parents to apply them to home situations. The additional resources included in the treatment manual enable users to experience the full value of CPRT."

—**Louise Guerney, PhD, RPT-S**, professor emerita at Penn State University, co-developer of Filial Therapy, and faculty member of the National Institute of Relationship Enhancement (NIRE)

Child-Parent Relationship Therapy (CPRT) Treatment Manual

This newly expanded and revised edition of the *Child-Parent Relationship Therapy (CPRT) Treatment Manual* is the essential companion to the second edition of *Child-Parent Relationship Therapy (CPRT)*. The second edition is updated to include four new CPRT treatment protocols and parent notebooks adapted for specific populations: parents of toddlers, parents of preadolescents, adoptive families, and the teacher/student relationship, along with the revised original CPRT protocol and parent notebook for ages 3–10.

This manual provides the CPRT/filial therapist with a comprehensive framework for conducting CPRT. Included are detailed outlines, teaching aids, activities, and resources for each of the 10 sessions. The manual is divided into two major sections, *Therapist Protocol* and *Parent Notebook*, and contains a comprehensive *CPRT Training Resources* section along with an index to the accompanying *Companion Website*.

The accompanying *Companion Website* contains all necessary and supplemental training materials in a format that allows for ease of reproduction and enhanced usability including the following:

- **CPRT Protocol—Ages 3 to 10** and **Parent Notebook**
- **Toddler Adapted CPRT Protocol** and **Parent Notebook**
- **Preadolescent Adapted CPRT Protocol** and **Parent Notebook**
- **Adoptive Families Adapted CPRT Protocol** and **Parent Notebook**
- **Teacher-Student Adapted Protocol** and **Teacher Notebook**
- **Therapist Study Guide**
- **Training Resources, Teaching Aids** and **Supplemental Materials**
- **Marketing Materials**
- **Assessments**

Drawing on their extensive experience as professional play therapists and filial therapists, Bratton and Landreth apply the principles of CCPT and CPRT in this easy-to-follow protocol for practitioners to successfully implement the evidence-based CPRT model. By using this manual and the accompanying *Companion Website* in conjunction with the CPRT text, filial therapists will have a complete package for training parents in CCPT skills to act as therapeutic agents with their own children.

Sue C. Bratton, PhD, LPC-S, RPT-S, is professor emerita, department of counseling and higher education, and director emerita, Center for Play Therapy at the University of North Texas.

Garry L. Landreth, EdD, LPC, RPT-S, is regents professor emeritus, department of counseling and higher education, and founder and director emeritus, Center for Play Therapy at the University of North Texas.

Child-Parent Relationship Therapy (CPRT) Treatment Manual

An Evidence-Based 10-Session Filial Therapy Model

2nd Edition

Sue C. Bratton and
Garry L. Landreth

Routledge
Taylor & Francis Group
NEW YORK AND LONDON

Second edition published 2020
by Routledge
52 Vanderbilt Avenue, New York, NY 10017

and by Routledge
2 Park Square, Milton Park, Abingdon, Oxon, OX14 4RN

Routledge is an imprint of the Taylor & Francis Group, an informa business

First edition published by Routledge 2006

Library of Congress Cataloging-in-Publication Data
A catalog record for this book has been requested

ISBN: 978-1-138-68894-0 (pbk)
ISBN: 978-1-315-53798-6 (ebk)

Typeset in Garamond
by Apex CoVantage, LLC

Visit the Companion Website: www.routledge.com/cw/bratton

Printed and bound by CPI Group (UK) Ltd, Croydon, CR0 4YY

Contents

Note: All Materials in this Treatment Manual as well as full versions of all 5 CPRT Therapist Protocols and the corresponding Parent Notebooks, Therapist Study Guide, and supplemental materials and resources are available on the Companion Website at www.routledge.com/cw/bratton

Acknowledgments

The rewarding shared opportunity with our spouses, Monica and David, to be parents is the most significant experience in which we have invested our lives. Our children, Kimberly, Karla, and Craig (G.L.L.) and Lauren (S.C.B.), have made the journey through parenting a wonderful experience as we have struggled to live out the principles of Child-Parent Relationship Therapy on a daily basis with them. They have reaffirmed our faith in the process. This book is dedicated to Monica and David, our children, and our grandchildren. Without their inspiration, love, and encouragement, this book would not have been possible.

We would also like to acknowledge the contributions of our graduate students, whose enthusiasm about CPRT and its positive impact on families has been a significant factor in writing this book. We are especially grateful to our many doctoral students who have contributed to the research on the effectiveness of this model. A special thanks to our contributing authors, Mary Morrison Bennett, Kara Carnes-Holt, Peggy Ceballos, Wendy Pretz Helker, Kristin Meany-Walen, and Kristie Opiola, whose experience and expertise in their topic areas provide a significant addition to the second edition. We are also indebted to Lauren Dimon, Alyssa Swan, and Rinda Thomas-Stein for assistance in preparing and editing the manuscript. Finally, we wish to acknowledge and thank Theresa Kellam and Sandy Blackard for their inspiration, contributions, and feedback throughout the process of writing the first edition of this manual and for their contribution to the Study Guide on the Companion Website.

Contributors

Mary Morrison Bennett, PhD, LPC-S, RPT-S, is a Fellow, Institute for Play Therapy at Texas State University and in private practice in Austin, Tx.

Kara Carnes-Holt, PhD, LPC, RPT-S, is associate professor, school of counseling, leadership advocacy, and design, and founder and director, Rocky Mountain Center of Play Therapy Studies at the University of Wyoming.

Peggy L. Ceballos, PhD, NCC, is associate professor and school counseling coordinator, department of counseling and higher education, University of North Texas

Wendy P. Helker, PhD, LPC-S, RPT-S, is Certified School Counselor and adjunct faculty, department of counseling and higher education, University of North Texas.

Kristin K. Meany-Walen, PhD, LMHC, RPT-S, is Mental Health Coordinator, Waterloo Community School District, Iowa and adjunct faculty at University of Northern Iowa.

Kristie K. Opiola, PhD, LPC, RPT, is assistant professor, department of counseling and higher education at the University of North Carolina at Charlotte.

Getting Started

OVERVIEW OF THE CPRT TREATMENT MANUAL CONTENTS AND USE

The ***Child-Parent Relationship Therapy (CPRT) Treatment Manual: An Evidence-Based 10-Session Filial Therapy Model, 2nd Edition***, is a companion to the textbook *Child-Parent Relationship Therapy (CPRT): An Evidence-Based 10-Session Filial Therapy Model* (Landreth & Bratton, 2020), available from the publisher, Routledge. The CPRT Protocol is an evidence-based protocol intended for use by mental health professionals trained and certified in the CPRT model (https://cpt.unt.edu/child-parent-relationship-therapy-certification). Permission to copy training materials is granted to the therapist in conjunction with the purchase of this manual for personal use only. The copyright statement must appear on each page.

The training materials included in this manual assume the reader is familiar with the information contained in the textbook. The textbook contains information essential to conducting CPRT including developmental and cultural considerations and interpersonal neurobiology concepts relevant to CPRT. This manual is designed to be helpful to therapists with all levels of experience.

The ***CPRT Treatment Manual*** has two major sections, *Therapist Protocol for Ages 3–10* and *Parent Notebook for Ages 3–10*, and contains a comprehensive *CPRT Training Resources* section along with an index to the accompanying Companion Website. The Companion Website found at www.routledge.com/cw/bratton contains the 10-session *CPRT Study Guide*, *Appendices* containing supplemental training materials, clinical forms, organizational tools, assessments, and marketing materials, as well as the electronic version of the *Therapist Protocol for Ages 3–10*, *Parent Notebook for Ages 3–10*, and **four new protocols designed to help therapists respond to the specific needs of parents of toddlers, parents of preadolescents, adoptive families, and teacher-student relationships**. The complete *Therapist Protocol* and the corresponding *Parent/Teacher Notebook* for each of the four new protocols are downloaded from the Companion Website. The electronic files allow the therapist to print the necessary training materials for each new CPRT group. Unlike many commercially available parent training programs, there are no additional books or materials that must be purchased to conduct CPRT.

The ***Therapist Protocol*** for each of the five CPRT protocols is organized by sessions and contains all materials required to conduct the 10-session CPRT model, including Treatment Outlines for Sessions 1–10 and all corresponding parent handouts, homework, and parent worksheets. The *Therapist Protocol* contains copies of all handouts in the *Parent Notebook*—with sample answers for the therapist. Sample answers are provided only as an example of an appropriate response that is consistent with the Child-Centered Play Therapy (CCPT) philosophy. For additional CCPT skills and responses, refer to Chapter 6, "CPRT Skills, Concepts, and Attitudes to Be Taught," in the companion CPRT text (Landreth & Bratton, 2019).

Prior to conducting CPRT, therapists download and print the 10-session *Therapist Protocol* from the accompanying Companion Website. This method allows therapists to print new protocols as needed. We have found that using a three-ring binder with pocket dividers and tabs for each of the 10 sessions is an efficient and useful method of organizing the materials. In preparation for each parent training session:

- Print the Materials Checklist (Appendix A) several days ahead to allow time to gather materials, videos, books, etc.
- Review the *Study Guide* (Appendix B) for the respective session. The Study Guide is designed with the novice CPRT therapist in mind.
- Review the CPRT demonstration video featuring Drs. Landreth and Bratton illustrating the delivery and process of the CPRT model with four couples (source referenced in Chapter VIII), and the session transcripts provided in the companion text (Landreth & Bratton, 2019). These resources illustrate the delivery of the CPRT curriculum and the delicate balance of presenting didactic content with group process and experiential activities.
- Be familiar with the organization of the Parent Notebook and page numbers of handouts, so that you can quickly refer parents to a specific handout or assignment during the weekly sessions.

The CPRT protocol is designed to be flexible to help you adapt the training to the unique needs of parents and children. As noted in the CPRT text (Landreth & Bratton, 2019), the 10-session curriculum presented in this manual can be adapted for use in fewer sessions, as well as extended for a longer number of sessions, depending on parent needs and group size. Although designed for use with groups of parents, the materials are also easily adapted for use with individual parents and couples. As with any treatment/intervention, therapists are expected to ***exercise clinical judgment*** in the use of materials and procedures.

The ***Parent Notebook*** for each of the five CPRT protocols includes all the printed materials that parents will need to complete CPRT training. For ease of duplication and to ensure correct pagination, *Parent Notebooks* are printed from the accompanying Companion Website found at www.routledge.com/cw/bratton. The website version of each *Parent Notebook* is formatted for two-sided printing with blank pages inserted where needed so that each new session begins on odd numbered page. We suggest organizing the notebook into a three-brad pocket folder or small three-ring binder with 1–10 tabs to designate the 10 sessions. Other useful strategies for the organization of training materials include printing the most-used handouts, *Play Session Dos and Don'ts, Play Session Procedures Checklist, and CPRT Cliff Notes* on different colors of paper or using tabs to provide an easy method for parents to locate them in their notebooks. Note: The Parent Notebooks and marketing materials in the Companion Website refer to CPRT as Child-Parent-Relationship (C-P-R) Training for Parents (designation used by Landreth in the early development of the model), whereas all therapist materials retain the title Child-Parent Relationship Therapy (CPRT), the formal name of the model.

Handouts in the *Parent Notebook* are organized by the CPRT training session they are typically used in. Some flexibility in presenting materials is allowed, depending on the needs of a particular group of parents. *Appendix A* in the Companion Website contains additional resources that the therapist can print and provide to parents. Supplemental skill practice worksheets for parents are also included in *Appendix D*. Although these supplemental worksheets are provided as additional practice for CPRT skills that a particular group of parents may be having difficulty with, the therapist is cautioned to avoid overwhelming parents with too much information or homework. Again, it is expected that the therapist will **exercise clinical judgment** in determining when and if to use supplemental materials.

CPRT Training Resources includes a list of useful resources for professionals and parents. Resources are organized by videos, books, and manuals. Each of those categories is further divided into recommended and supplemental resources.

Appendix A includes helpful organizational and practical materials for CPRT training. These materials are prepared for ease of reprinting for each new group and include (a) *Parent Information Form* to complete prior to Session 1 and to note important information about group participants. This form should be brought to every session; therefore we suggest inserting it in the front of the *Therapist Protocol;* (b) the *Materials Checklist* for Sessions 1–10 to help therapists know what to bring to each session; the therapist is advised to bring a few extras of all printed materials that parents will need for each session, in the likely case a parent forgets the *Parent Notebook*; (c) *CPRT Progress Notes* to document the clinical progress of individual group members throughout Sessions 1–10; and the (d) *Therapist Skills Checklist* for the novice CPRT therapist or student intern for supervision purposes and to self-assess important CPRT skills. This appendix also contains items for parents that are to be handed out separately from the *Parent Notebook* materials, including *Homemade Playdough and Paint Recipes, Special Playtime Appointment Cards, "Do Not Disturb" Template*, and *Certificates of Completion.*

Appendix B contains the *Study Guide* and is designed for the beginning CPRT therapist to review prior to each CPRT training session. It is not intended for use during the CPRT sessions. The *Study Guide* is an expanded version of the *Therapist Protocol* and is designed to provide a more in-depth explanation of content. This section begins with "Helpful Hints for Conducting CPRT" followed by the expanded Treatment Outlines for each session. Embedded within each Treatment Outline are shaded text boxes with additional information and examples for each training concept or activity to aid you in preparing for each session. The material in the shaded text boxes is not meant to be presented in full or memorized. In several cases, the authors have shared personal parenting experiences to illustrate a point, but it is important to use your own stories and metaphors, making teaching points in a way that feels comfortable and congruent. If you are not a parent and have little personal experience with children, do not try to pretend that you do. You can draw on your professional experience as a play therapist, teacher, and so forth, or share stories of friends' or relatives' experiences with children. For the experienced CPRT therapist, the *Study Guide* can serve as a brief review.

We suggest that therapists have the *Therapist Protocol* at hand when reviewing the *Study Guide* in preparation for each session, making any additional notes directly on the Treatment Outline for that session. **Never use the *Study Guide* during CPRT sessions**; training should not be scripted. The CPRT curriculum is designed to be used by experienced play therapists with prior training, experience, and certification in both Child-Centered Play Therapy and CPRT, as well as training and experience in facilitating group therapy. This training and experience base is necessary in order to facilitate a lively, spontaneous, and interactive group training process. Reading from the *Study Guide* would interfere with this process and impede the development of a therapeutic connection between the parents and therapist. The therapist should become familiar enough with the material in the *Study Guide* to deliver the training in his or her own unique way of engaging parents in the treatment process. As noted earlier, it is expected that the therapist will exercise clinical judgment in using these materials in order to best meet the specific needs of a particular group of parents. Note: It is also necessary to refer to the *Materials Checklist* (see Appendix A in the Companion Website) as you prepare for each training session.

Appendix C includes a poster format of the most frequently used handout, *Play Session Dos and Don'ts*, formatted so that the therapist can print it out on three colored sheets of 8½" × 11" paper, tape it together, and laminate it as a poster to provide a handy visual for referencing these important skills during Sessions 3–10.

Appendix D includes supplemental parent handouts and worksheets with therapist versions containing example answers. The supplemental handouts provide opportunities for additional practice of CPRT skills and are used at the discretion of the therapist's assessment of the parents' needs. The session numbers on each worksheet corresponds to when that particular skill is generally introduced or practiced. Worksheets include Feelings Response Practice for Session 2, Choice Giving 101 for Session 6, Esteem-Building Responses for Session 7, Encouragement vs. Praise for Session 8, and Advanced Limit Setting: Giving Choices as Consequences for Noncompliance for Session 9. There is also a handout on *Structured Doll Play*. References to these optional worksheets are included in the Study Guide for the sessions in which we recommend their use; however, they may be used flexibly, depending on the needs of a particular group of parents. Although these supplemental worksheets are provided as additional practice for CPRT skills that a particular group of parents may be struggling to implement, the therapist is cautioned to avoid overwhelming parents with too much information or homework. Again, it is expected that the therapist will exercise clinical judgment in determining when and if to use supplemental materials.

Appendix E includes information for successful marketing of CPRT to parents. Sample flyers and brochure are included. These materials may be electronically adapted for therapist use. Note: The acronym C-P-R Training is used on all marketing materials for parents as well as materials that they receive in their parent notebooks.

Appendix F includes three unpublished assessments that have been used for research in CPRT and filial therapy: *Porter Parental Acceptance Scale* (PPAS), *Filial Problems Checklist* (FPC), and *Measurement of Empathy in Adult-Child Interaction* (MEACI). All three measures are designed to be administered pre and post treatment. The PPAS and FPC are self-report instruments administered to parents; the PPAS measures the parents' attitude of acceptance toward the child of focus, while the FPC measures the parents' perception of the child of focus's behavior. The MEACI is a direct observational measure of parental empathy that requires pre and post video-recording of parents (the use of this instrument requires substantial training and inter-rater reliability). Instruments and scoring are included in separate files for ease of printing. We gratefully acknowledge Dr. Louise Guerney and Dr. Blaine Porter for generously allowing us to include these materials for use by CPRT therapists.

The CPRT Treatment Manual also contains a Companion Website to allow the therapist to easily print the required CPRT training materials (*Therapist Protocol* and *Parent Notebook*). The Companion Website also includes the *CPRT Study Guide* and several useful appendices not found in the manual. The appendices contain organizational materials, clinical forms, marketing materials, assessments, and supplemental skill practice worksheets for parents.

Note: Permission to copy the materials is granted to the therapist in conjunction with the purchase of this training. The copyright statement should be printed out and included on all copied materials.

Helpful Hints for Conducting CPRT

The following tips are excerpts from Chapter 5: "Critical Components in Facilitating the Process of CPRT" in Child-Parent Relationship Therapy (CPRT): An Evidence-Based 10-Session Filial Therapy Model, 2nd Edition *(Landreth & Bratton, 2019).*

The CPRT process is characterized by **two key components: a didactic component and a group process component in the context of a safe, reassuring, supportive, and nonthreatening environment** that encourages parents to explore feelings, attitudes, and perceptions about themselves, their children, and about parenting.

The supportive format in a CPRT group often resembles group therapy as the therapist responds empathically to parents' issues and emotional reactions related to their family or their role as parents. Likening the emotional exploring and supportive component of CPRT to group therapy does not imply that the objective is to provide group therapy, only that some aspects of the group interaction and process take on the nature of group therapy for short periods of time as parents explore their feelings about themselves, their children, and their families. The transition from this empathic group therapy type element of exploring an emotional issue to the didactic element can be accomplished by limiting the group therapy exploration to a few minutes of interaction, making an empathic reflection that summarizes the parents' feelings, and then making a teaching point that is related to the content of the parents' sharing.

Processing parents' reactions and feelings about their children promotes the beginning of change in parents' perceptions about their children. The CPRT therapist must maintain a delicate balance between the didactic and process dimensions without being rigid in covering the scheduled training material or allowing the group to become bogged down in the group therapy dimensions of the process.

It is imperative that the therapist intersperse the teaching component of CPRT with building **group cohesiveness**, especially in the first two or three training sessions. This is accomplished when the therapist generalizes parent disclosures to help parents identify with each other by asking questions: "Does this sound familiar to anyone else?" or "Anyone else ever yell at your child?" and "What was that like for you?" when a parent responds affirmatively. When parents nod their heads understandingly as a parent describes a problem, the therapist can comment: "So the rest of you know what that is like." This **linking of parents** helps break down barriers of isolation and the feeling, "I'm the only one who feels this way" or "I'm the only one who ever yells at her child."

If a parent describes a point of difficulty in a play session, the therapist can ask, "Group, what Rule of Thumb applies here?" The therapist can also encourage group interaction by inviting parents to respond to each other's questions: "Linda, how would you suggest Erika respond when her son wants to paint her glasses?" This question not only facilitates interaction, but also decreases parents' dependence on the therapist for solutions by inviting parents to contribute their ideas. If a parent seems to be thoughtful about something, the therapist can invite sharing: "Angela, what are you thinking?" The guiding principle for the therapist is careful adherence to the **Rule of Thumb: The therapist is a facilitator of interaction, not just a trainer.** An objective is that, as the training progresses, the interaction among the parents will increase, and they will be more actively supportive and offer suggestions to one another.

The following teaching components should be observed in conducting the training sessions:

- Presenting the information to be learned in **simple, concise teaching points** is the key to parents learning and assimilating new information.
- Remember the **3 Ds: Describe, Demonstrate, and Do**. Therapists first **describe** and teach the skill, next **demonstrate** the skill (video or live), then ask the parents to **do**—role-play what they saw you do.
- **Simple homework assignments** and concise informational handouts are provided to reinforce teaching points made in the training sessions.
- **Active affirmation** of parents' efforts is considered to be a critical key to the effectiveness of CPRT.
- Employing a variety of teaching tools such as **stories, analogies, and metaphors to emphasize teaching points** helps to maintain a high level of parent interest and facilitates the learning process. Parents may have difficulty recalling a teaching point in isolation, but when the point is attached to a short interest-catching story, parents will remember the story and, in turn, the teaching point.
- Catchy **"Rules of Thumb"** also help make teaching points easier for parents to remember.
- The therapist's responses to parents should consistently **model basic Child-Centered Play Therapy principles and skills**.
- The therapist can **use self-disclosure** about his or her efforts and mistakes as a parent to illustrate teaching points and to model permission to make mistakes.

- Modeling is also utilized by **showing videos of the therapist's play sessions** or by the therapist conducting a live play session to demonstrate the kind of responses hoped for by parents in their play sessions.
- When viewing the video of a parent's play session, the video should be stopped frequently to validate and affirm the parent's efforts. **The focus is on what the parents are doing correctly** rather than focusing on mistakes.

We hope that you find this manual helpful and informative.

Sue and Garry

Note: For information on CPRT training workshops and Certification as a CPRT Practitioner and Practitioner-Supervisor, please contact the Center for Play Therapy, cpt.unt.edu, or contact Garry and Sue at sue.bratton@unt.edu

CHILD-PARENT RELATIONSHIP THERAPY (CPRT) AGES 3–10

THERAPIST PROTOCOL

Treatment Outlines and Handouts for Sessions 1–10

Using the CPRT Therapist Protocol for Ages 3–10

The CPRT Protocol for ages 3–10 is an evidence-based protocol intended for use by mental health professionals trained and certified in the CPRT model (https://cpt.unt.edu/child-parent-relationship-therapy-certification). *Note: We have included four new protocols in this second edition designed to help therapists respond to the specific needs of parents of toddlers, parents of preadolescents, adoptive families, and teacher–student relationships. The complete Therapist Protocol and the corresponding Parent/Teacher Notebook for each of the four new protocols are downloaded from the accompanying Companion Website.*

CPRT practitioners are expected to download the *Therapist Protocol—Ages 3–10* from the Companion Website found at www.routledge.com/cw/bratton, rather than copy from this manual, and familiarize themselves with the organization and content prior to conducting CPRT. The *CPRT Therapist Protocol* is organized by sessions and contains all materials required to conduct the 10-session CPRT model, including Treatment Outlines for Sessions 1–10 and all corresponding parent handouts, homework, and parent worksheets. The *Therapist Protocol—Ages 3–10* contains copies of all handouts found in the *Parent Notebook for Ages 3–10* and provides sample answers for the therapist. Sample answers are provided only as an example of an appropriate response that is consistent with the Child-Centered Play Therapy (CCPT) philosophy. For additional CCPT skills and responses, refer to Chapter 6, "CPRT Skills, Concepts, and Attitudes to Be Taught," in the companion CPRT text (Landreth & Bratton, 2019).

Downloading and printing the *Therapist Protocol for Ages 3–10* from the Companion Website allows for ease of reproduction and correct pagination. Therapists can easily print new protocols as needed. We have found that using a three-ring binder with pocket dividers and tabs for each of the 10 sessions is an efficient and useful method of organizing the materials. In preparation for each parent training session:

- Print the Materials Checklist (Appendix A) several days ahead to allow time to gather materials, videos, books, etc.
- Review the *Study Guide* (Appendix B) for that session. The Study Guide is designed with the novice CPRT therapist in mind.
- Review the CPRT demonstration video, CPRT in Action with four couples (Bratton & Landreth, 2014) and the detailed transcripts from actual CPRT Sessions 1–10 provided in the companion text (Landreth & Bratton, 2019). These resources illustrate the delivery of the CPRT curriculum and the delicate balance of presenting didactic content with group process and experiential activities.
- Print *Parent Notebooks* from the accompanying Companion Website. Be familiar with the organization of the Parent Notebook and page numbers of handouts, so that you can quickly refer parents to a specific handout or assignment during the weekly sessions.

The CPRT protocol is designed to be flexible to help you adapt the training to the unique needs of parents and children. As noted in the CPRT text (Landreth & Bratton, 2019), the 10-session curriculum presented in this manual can be adapted for use in fewer sessions, as well as extended for a longer number of sessions, depending on parent needs and group size. Although designed for use with groups of parents, the materials are also easily adapted for use with individual parents and couples. As with any treatment/intervention, therapists are expected to ***exercise clinical judgment*** in the use of materials and procedures.

Child-Parent Relationship Therapy (CPRT)

Session 1—Treatment Outline

⌚ Time Marker

Note: ***See Companion Website (www.routledge.com/cw/bratton)*** *to download and print Therapist Protocol—Session 1–10 and Parent Notebook—Sessions 1–10. Appendix A contains the Materials Checklist for this session, along with any additional materials for Session 1. The CPRT Training Resources Section in this manual provides information about suggested books and videos. For the experienced CPRT practitioner, the Treatment Outlines provide a suggested order for didactic components and allow for flexibility based on clinical judgment. The novice CPRT therapist is expected to refer to the Study Guide found in Appendix B in the Companion Website.*

________ **I. Give Name Tags and Parent Notebooks to All Parents as They Arrive**

(Ask parents who need to complete intake information to stay afterward.)

- Introduce yourself/co-leader and welcome parents to group!
- Facilitate brief parent introductions.
- Help parents feel supported and not alone in their parenting struggles.

________ **II. Overview of CPRT Training Objectives and Essential Concepts**

Note: Strive to weave-in training objectives and concepts in response to parents' questions and sharing concerns, rather than teaching in a linear way,

- **Rule of Thumb: "Focus on the donut, not the hole!"**
  (Optional: Bring in glazed donuts for parents and illustrate this concept in a creative way.)

  CPRT focuses on the relationship, your strengths, and your child's strengths (the dough; what's there)—not on the problem (the hole; what's missing).

- Play is the child's language.

  Play provides opportunities for your child to express thoughts, feelings, and wishes.

- CPRT helps *prevent* problems because parents become aware of child's emotional and relational needs.

- **Rule of Thumb: "Be a thermostat, not a thermometer!"**
  (Process briefly as group: What does a thermostat do; a thermometer?)

  You will learn to RESPOND rather than REACT. Your child's feelings are not your feelings and needn't escalate with your child's.

  The best way to calm your child is to first calm and center yourself (Perry & Szalavitz, 2006).

  Remember: In-control parents are thermostats; out-of-control parents are thermometers!

- You will learn basic play therapy skills that graduate students learn in a semester course.

These skills will:

- Return control to you as a parent and help your child to develop self-control.
- Promote secure attachment and provide closer, happier times with your child—more laughter, joy, and warm memories.

  "What do you want your child to remember about you/your relationship 20 years from now?" (Process as group: what are parents' best memories from childhood?)

- Give you the key to your child's inner world—learn how to really understand your child and communicate this understanding to your child.

- "Best of all—you only have to practice these new skills and do something different for 30 minutes per week!"
- Reminder: Patience is an important component of learning this new "play language."
- ***"In 10 weeks, you are going to be different, and your relationship with your child will be different."***

______ III. Group Introductions

(Goal: Facilitate sharing and connection between parents.)

- Invite each parent to describe his/her entire family (help parents select a child of focus if not identified during intake).
- Take notes on *Parent Information Form* as parents share blessings and concerns about their child of focus.
- Make normalizing/generalizing comments to link parents as they each share.

  Example: ***"Anyone else feel angry/frustrated with their child this week?"***

- **Rule of Thumb: "What's most important may not be what you did, but what you do *after* what you have done!"**

  We are all certain to make mistakes, but we can recover. It is how we handle our mistakes that makes the difference.

  In this way, parents offer children a model of how to repair relationships!

______ IV. Reflective Responding

- A way of following rather than leading during the 30-minute playtimes.
- Reflect behaviors, thoughts, needs/wishes, and feelings (without asking questions).

  If you know enough to ask a question, you know enough to make a reflection.

- Helps the parent understand the child and helps the child feel understood.

"Be-With" Attitudes Convey:	**Not:**
I am here; I hear you.	I always agree.
I understand.	I must make you happy.
I care.	I will solve your problems.

_______ **V. Optional—Show Video Clips of *Life's First Feelings*** (see Training Resources)

- Video clip #1: Watch; discuss what parents notice in "typical" interaction and what they notice about the baby in the "Still Face" experiment.

  In the typical interaction (parent-child dance), notice co-regulation process and how the baby depends on the parent to stay connected in the relationship.

  As parents, how often are we focused on a task or the phone and miss opportunities for connection with our children?

- Video clip #2: Watch; discuss parents' reactions to universal feelings and how feelings are shown in the babies' faces (especially mad-sad).

_______ **VI. Feelings Response: In-Class Practice Worksheet** (*Parent Notebook* p. 128). Complete worksheet together with parents.

- Ask parents as a group to decide on feeling words that best describe how the child in each scenario is feeling.
- Then, as a group, decide on a short reflective response.

______ **VII. Role-play** (Goal: Parents actively practice reflective responding)

- Ask a parent to tell you about their day for 30 seconds (or demonstrate with co-leader) and at the end of 30 seconds, simply reflect what you heard.
- Then, pair up parents and ask them to take turns being the "listener" practicing reflective responding.

_____ **VIII. Optional—Video Demonstration** (if time permits)

- Show a video clip of an example play session demonstrating skills of reflection of feeling and allowing the child to lead.

_______ **IX. Homework Assignments** (*Parent Notebook* p. 127)

☐ Practice reflective responding—complete *Feelings Response: Homework Worksheet* and bring to group next week.

☐ Notice one physical characteristic about your child you haven't seen before.

- ☐ Bring your favorite, heart-tugging photo of your child of focus.
- ☐ Practice giving a *30-second Burst of Attention*.
  Example: If you are on the telephone, say, "Can you hold for 30 seconds? I'll be right back." Put the phone aside, bend down, and give your child undivided, focused attention for 30 seconds; then say "I have to finish talking to ______." Stand back up and continue talking with your friend.

______ **X. Close with Motivational Poem, Story, or Rule of Thumb (optional)**

Suggest: *I'll Love You Forever* by Robert Munsch or other children's books and resources included in the *CPRT Training Resources* section of this manual

---

RULES OF THUMB TO REMEMBER:

1. **"Focus on the donut, not the hole!"** Focus on the relationship, NOT the problem.
2. **"Be a thermostat, not a thermometer."** Learn to RESPOND (reflect) rather than REACT.
3. **"What's most important may not be what you do, but what you do after what you have done!"** We all make mistakes, but we can recover. It is how we handle our mistakes that makes the difference.

CHILD-PARENT-RELATIONSHIP (C-P-R) TRAINING
Parent Notes and Homework—Session 1

RULES OF THUMB TO REMEMBER:

1. **"Focus on the donut, not the hole!"** Focus on the Relationship, NOT the Problem.
2. **"Be a thermostat, not a thermometer."** Learn to RESPOND (reflect) rather than REACT.

   Remember: The best way to calm your child is to first calm and center yourself.
3. **"What's most important may not be what you do, but what you do after what you have done!"** We all make mistakes, but we can recover. It is how we handle our mistakes that makes the difference.

Reflective Responding:

A way of following, rather than leading.

Reflect behaviors, thoughts, needs/wishes, and feelings (without asking questions).

Helps you understand your child and helps your child feel understood.

"Be-With" Attitudes Convey:	**Not:**
I am here; I hear you.	I always agree.
I understand.	I must make you happy.
I care.	I will solve your problems.

Notes: (use back for additional notes)

____

____

____

____

____

Homework Assignments:

- ☐ Practice reflective responding (complete *Feeling Response: Homework Worksheet* and bring next week).

  ____
- ☐ Notice one physical characteristic about your child you haven't seen before.
- ☐ Bring your favorite, heart-tugging picture of your child of focus.
- ☐ Practice giving a 30-second Burst of Attention. If you are on the telephone, say, "Can you hold for 30 seconds? I'll be right back." Put the phone aside, bend down, and give your child undivided, focused attention for 30 seconds; then say, "I have to finish talking to ____________." Stand back up and continue talking with your friend.

CHILD-PARENT-RELATIONSHIP (C-P-R) TRAINING
Feelings Response: In-Class Practice Worksheet—Session 1

Directions: (1) Look into child's eyes for clue to feeling. (2) After you've decided what child is feeling, put the feeling word into a short response, generally beginning with you, "you seem sad" or "you're really mad at me right now." (3) Your facial expression and tone of voice should match your child's (empathy is conveyed more through non-verbals than verbals).

Child: Oscar is telling you all the things he's going to show his older cousin, Sophia, this weekend.

Child Felt: Excited, Happy

Parent Response: You're excited to play with Sophia!

Child: Serena gets in the car after school and tells you that Bert, the class pet hamster, died—and then tells you about how she was in charge of feeding Bert last week and how he would look at her and then get on his wheel and run.

Child Felt: Sad, Disappointed

Parent Response: You're sad that Bert died.

Child: Andre was playing with his friend, Harry, when Harry grabbed Andre's fire truck and wouldn't give it back. Andre tried to get it back and the ladder broke off. Andre comes to you crying and tells you what happened and that it's all Harry's fault.

Child Felt: Mad, Angry, Upset

Parent Response: You're really mad at Harry or You're really upset about your truck.

Child: Zara was playing in the garage while you were cleaning it out, when a big box of books falls off the shelf and hits the floor behind her. She jumps up and runs over to you.

Child Felt: Scared, Surprised (depends on child's facial expression)

Parent Response: That (scared, surprised. . .) you!

CHILD-PARENT-RELATIONSHIP (C-P-R) TRAINING
Feelings Response: Homework Worksheet—Session 1

Directions: (1) Look into child's eyes for clue to feeling. (2) After you've decided what child is feeling, put the feeling word into a short response, generally beginning with you, "you seem sad" or "you're really mad at me right now."
(3) Remember the importance of your facial expression and tone of voice matching child's (empathy is conveyed more through non-verbals than verbals).

Child: (what happened/what child did or said)

____

____

____

Child Felt: ______________________________

Parent Response: ______________________________

____

____

Alternate Response (if needed): ______________________________

____

____

Child: (what happened/what child did or said)

____

____

____

Child Felt: ______________________________

Parent Response: ______________________________

____

____

Alternate Response (if needed): ______________________________

____

____

Child: (what happened/what child did or said)

____

____

____

Child Felt: ______________________________

Parent Response: ______________________________

____

____

Alternate Response (if needed): ______________________________

____

____

Child: (what happened/what child did or said)

____

____

____

Child Felt: ______________________________

Parent Response: ______________________________

____

____

Alternate Response (if needed): ______________________________

____

____

CHILD-PARENT-RELATIONSHIP (C-P-R) TRAINING
What Is It and How Can It Help?

What Is It?

Child-Parent-Relationship (C-P-R) Training is a special 10-session parent training program to help strengthen the relationship between a parent and a child by using 30-minute playtimes once a week. Play is the most natural way children communicate. Toys are like words for children and play is their language. Adults talk about their experiences, thoughts, and feelings. Children use toys to explore their experiences and express what they think and how they feel. Therefore, parents are taught to have special structured 30-minute playtimes with their child using a kit of carefully selected toys in their own home. Parents learn how to respond empathically to their child's feelings, build their child's self-esteem, help their child learn self-control and self-responsibility, and set therapeutic limits during these special playtimes.

For 30 minutes each week, the child is the center of the parent's universe. In this special playtime, the parent creates an accepting relationship in which a child feels completely safe to express himself through his play—fears, likes, dislikes, wishes, anger, loneliness, joy, or feelings of failure. This is not a typical playtime. It is a special playtime in which the child leads and the parent follows. In this special relationship, there are no:

- reprimands
- put-downs
- evaluations
- requirements (to draw pictures a certain way, etc.)
- judgments (about the child or his play as being good or bad, right or wrong)

How Can It Help My Child?

In the special playtimes, you will build a different kind of relationship with your child, and your child will discover that she is capable, important, understood, and accepted as she is. When children experience a play relationship in which they feel accepted, understood, and cared for, they play out many of their problems and, in the process, release tensions, feelings, and burdens. Your child will then feel better about herself and will be able to discover her own strengths and assume greater self-responsibility as she takes charge of play situations.

How your child feels about herself will make a significant difference in her behavior. In the special playtimes where you learn to focus on your child rather than your child's problem, your child will begin to react differently, because how your child behaves, how she thinks, and how she performs in school are directly related to how she feels about herself. When your child feels better about herself, she will behave in more self-enhancing ways rather than self-defeating ways.

Child-Parent Relationship Therapy (CPRT)

Session 2—Treatment Outline

⏱ Time Marker

Note: ***See Companion Website*** *Appendix A to download and print Materials Checklist and any additional materials for this session. The CPRT Training Resources section in this manual provides information about suggested books and videos*

________ **I. Informal Sharing and Review of Homework**

- Check in about each parent's week and reflect briefly.
- Review homework from Session 1:
  - 30-second Burst of Attention
  - *Feelings Response: Homework Worksheet*—refer parents to worksheet to review and practice reflective responding. Reflect parents' experiences and model encouragement as parents share.
  - Physical Characteristic/Favorite Picture—invite parents to share. Reflect their emotions as they report noticing their child's characteristic and share their photos

________ **II. Demonstration of Toys: *Toy Checklist for Play Sessions*** handout (Bring toys for demonstration and for parents to use to role play in IV. Helpful to bring example filial toy kit)

- Briefly review Toy Categories on *Toy Checklist for Play Sessions* (*Parent Notebook* p. 132). Don't read the entire list.
- Demonstrate/show toys and briefly explain rationale—especially for toys that may concern parents (dart gun and baby bottle). You might ask parents: "What toys surprise you to see on the list?" Process their concerns.
- As toys are shown, briefly provide examples of how you might respond to child playing with that toy (co-leader can role-play with you!).
- Discuss finding inexpensive, used, or free toys to include in kit.
- Emphasize the importance of the toys. *Ask parents to commit to having over half the toys by next week—preferably all.* If they don't, they likely won't be ready for their first play session.
- Discuss pros and cons of involving child in collecting toys for play session kit.

_______ **III.** ***Basic Principles of Play Sessions*** handout (*Parent Notebook* p. 133)

Briefly review the Basic Principles with focus on **"Be-With" Attitudes**.

I'm here—I hear you—I understand—I care—I delight in you!

1. Parent allows the child to lead and parent follows, without asking questions or making suggestions.

- o Show keen interest and closely observe.
- o Body language conveys interest and full attention.
  (*Optional*: Spontaneously role-play with one parent in group what it is like to talk without giving parent full attention vs. what it is like to talk when receiving full attention/toes follow nose body language.)

  Rule of Thumb: "The parent's toes should follow their nose."

- o Actively join in when invited.
- o Parent is no longer a teacher; the child is "*expert*" for 30 minutes.

2. Parents' major task is to empathize with their child.

- o See and experience your child's play through your child's eyes.
- o Understand child's needs, feelings, and thoughts expressed through play.

3. Parents communicate this understanding to their child by:

- o Describing what the child is doing/playing.
- o Reflecting what the child is saying.
- o Reflecting what the child is feeling.

4. Parent is clear, firm, and consistent about the *few* "limits" that are placed on child's behavior during playtimes.

- o Parent gives child responsibility for behavior.
- o Limits are set for safety, to prevent breaking toys or damaging play area, and to end session.
- o Limits are used only when needed.

Note: If time allows, briefly review goals of play sessions on handout.

_______ **IV. Demonstration and Role-Play of Basic Play Session Skills**

- At least 10 minutes: Demonstrate (video or live) play skills, stopping to answer questions and process reactions.

- 10–15 minutes: Parents pair up and role-play with the toys, taking turns being a child and a parent practicing basic play session skills just demonstrated.
- 5–10 minutes: Therapist role-plays "scenarios" to which parents had difficulty responding during partner role-play.

Structuring for Success Tips:

Show video clip (never a client video) that clearly demonstrates the concept of setting the stage, allowing child to lead (without asking questions), tracking, and conveying **"Be-With" Attitudes** (or conduct live demo focusing on same attitudes and skills).

________ V. Choosing a Time and Place for Play Sessions

- Suggest a room that parent believes will offer the fewest distractions to the child and greatest freedom from worry about breaking things or making a mess.

  Example: Kitchen area is ideal if no one else at home; otherwise, choose a space where the door can be closed.

- Set aside a regular time in advance. This time is to be undisturbed—no phone calls or interruptions by other family members, and a time when the child is not tired or hungry.
- Most importantly, parents choose a time when they feel most relaxed, rested, and emotionally available to their child.

Rule of Thumb: "You can't give away that which you don't possess."
(*Analogy*: Oxygen mask on airplane—take care of yourself first, then your child.)

As your child's most significant caregiver, you are asked to give so much of yourself; often when you simply don't have the resources within you to meet the demands of parenting.

You can't extend patience and acceptance to your child if you can't first offer it to yourself.

________ VI. Homework Assignments (*Parent Notebook* p. 131)

- ☐ Priority—Collect toys on *Toy Checklist for Play Sessions*. Brainstorm ideas and sources and suggest parents share resources.
- ☐ Select a consistent time and an uninterrupted place in the home suitable for the play sessions and report back next week. Set aside a regular time in advance.

  Day/Time: ____________________ ***Place:*** ______________________________

- ☐ Review *Basic Principles of Play Sessions* handout (*Parent Notebook* p. 133)
- ☐ Additional Assignment:

______ **VII. Close with Motivational Poem, Story, or Rule of Thumb** (optional)

👍 RULES OF THUMB TO REMEMBER:

1. **"The parent's toes should follow his/her nose."**
2. **"You can't give away that which you don't possess."** Remember the analogy of the oxygen mask on an airplane!

CHILD-PARENT-RELATIONSHIP (C-P-R) TRAINING
Parent Notes and Homework—Session 2

RULES OF THUMB TO REMEMBER:

1. **"The parent's toes should follow his/her nose."**
2. **"You can't give away that which you don't possess."** You can't extend patience and acceptance to your child if you can't first offer it to yourself. As your child's most significant caregiver, you are asked to give so much of yourself, often when you simply don't have the resources within you to meet the demands of parenting.

Remember the analogy of the oxygen mask on an airplane!

Focus on the "Be-With" Attitudes
I'm here—I hear you—I understand—I care—I delight in you!

Notes: (use back for additional notes)

____

____

____

____

____

____

____

____

Homework Assignments:

- ☐ Priority—Collect toys on *Toy Checklist for Play Sessions.*
- ☐ Select a consistent time and an uninterrupted place in the home suitable for the play sessions and report back next week—whatever room you feel offers the fewest distractions to the child and the greatest freedom from worry about breaking things or making a mess. Set aside a regular time in advance that is best for you and your child. This time is to be undisturbed—no phone calls or interruptions by other children.

Time: ________________ Place: ________________________________

- ☐ Review *Basic Principles of Play Sessions* handout
- ☐ Additional Assignment:

CHILD-PARENT-RELATIONSHIP (C-P-R) TRAINING
Toy Checklist for Play Sessions—Session 2

Note: Obtain sturdy cardboard box with lid or plastic container with lid to store toys (copy paper box is ideal—the deep lid becomes a dollhouse). Use an old blanket to spread toys out on and to serve as a boundary for the play area.

Real-Life Toys (also promote imaginative play)

- ☐ Small baby doll: *should not be anything "special"; can be extra one that child does not play with anymore*
- ☐ Baby bottle: *real one so it can be used by the child to put a drink in during the session*
- ☐ Doctor kit (with stethoscope): *add three Band-Aids for each session (add disposable gloves/Ace bandage, if you have)*
- ☐ Toy phones: *recommend getting two in order to communicate: one cell, one regular*
- ☐ Doll family: *bendable mother, father, brother, sister, baby, and so forth (representative of your family)*
- ☐ Play money: *bills and coins; credit card is optional*
- ☐ Couple of domestic and wild animals: *if you don't have doll family, you can substitute an animal family (e.g., horse, cow family)*
- ☐ Car/truck: *one to two small ones (could make specific to child's needs, e.g., an ambulance)*
- ☐ Kitchen dishes: *couple of plastic dishes, cups, and eating utensils*

Optional

- ☐ Small dollhouse: *use lid of box the toys are stored in—draw room divisions, windows, doors, and so forth inside of lid*
- ☐ Puppets: *one aggressive, one gentle; can be homemade or purchased (animal-shaped cooking mittens, etc.)*
- ☐ Doll furniture: *for a bedroom, bathroom, and kitchen*
- ☐ Dress up: *hand mirror, bandana, scarf; small items you already have around the house*

Acting-Out Aggressive Toys (also promote imaginative play)

- ☐ Dart guns with a couple of darts and a target: *parent needs to know how to operate*
- ☐ Rubber knife: *small, bendable, army type*
- ☐ Rope: *prefer soft rope (can cut the ends off jump rope)*
- ☐ Aggressive animal: *(e.g., snake, shark, lion, dinosaurs—strongly suggest hollow shark!)*
- ☐ Small toy soldiers (12–15): *two different colors to specify two teams or good guys/bad guys*
- ☐ Inflatable bop bag (Bobo *clown style preferable)*
- ☐ Mask: *Lone Ranger type*
- ☐ Toy handcuffs with a key

Toys for Creative/Emotional Expression

- ☐ Play-Doh: *suggest a cookie sheet or plastic placemat to put Play-Doh on to contain mess—also serves as a flat surface for drawing*
- ☐ Crayons: *eight colors, break some and peel paper off (markers are optional for older children but messier)*
- ☐ Plain paper: *provide a few pieces of new paper for each session*
- ☐ Scissors: *not pointed, but that cut well (e.g., child Fiskars*
- ☐ Transparent tape: *remember, child can use up all of this, so buy several of smaller size*
- ☐ Egg carton, styrofoam cup/bowl: *for destroying, breaking, or coloring*
- ☐ Ring toss game
- ☐ Soft foam ball
- ☐ Small musical instrument (preferably two)

Optional

- ☐ Selection of arts/crafts materials in a ziplock bag *(e.g., colored construction paper, glue, yarn, buttons, beads, scraps of fabrics, raw noodles, etc.—much of this depends on age of child)*
- ☐ Tinkertoys/small assortment of building blocks
- ☐ Binoculars
- ☐ Magic wand
- ☐ Two balloons (per play session)

***Reminder**: Toys need not be new or expensive. Avoid selecting more toys than will fit in a box—toys should be small. In some cases, additional toys can be added based on child's need and with therapist approval. If unable to get every toy before first play session, obtain several from each category—ask therapist for help in prioritizing.*

Note: Unwrap any new toys or take out of box before play session. Toys should look inviting.

Good Toy Hunting Places: garage sales, friends/relatives, "dollar" stores

CHILD-PARENT-RELATIONSHIP (C-P-R) TRAINING
Basic Principles of Play Sessions—Session 2

Basic Principles for Play Sessions:

1. The parent sets the stage by structuring an atmosphere in which the **child feels free** to determine how he will use the time during the 30-minute play session. The **child leads** the play and the **parent follows**. The parent follows the child's lead by showing keen interest and carefully observing the child's play, **without making suggestions or asking questions**, and by actively joining in the play when invited by the child. For 30 minutes, you (parent) are "dumb" and don't have the answers; it is up to your child to make his own decisions and find his own solutions. Your child is the expert.
2. The parent's major task is to empathize with the child: to understand the child's thoughts, feelings, and intent expressed in play by working hard to **see and experience the child's play through the child's eyes.** This task is operationalized by conveying the "Be-With" Attitudes below.
3. The parent is then to **communicate this understanding to the child** by (a) verbally describing what the child is doing/playing, (b) verbally reflecting what the child is saying, and (c) most importantly, by verbally reflecting the feelings that the child is actively experiencing through his play.
4. The parent is to be clear and firm about the few "limits" that are placed on the child's behavior. Limits are stated in a way that give the child responsibility for his actions and behaviors—helping to foster self-control. Limits to be set are time limits, not breaking toys or damaging items in the play area, and not physically hurting self or parent. **Limits are to be stated only when needed**, but applied consistently across sessions. (Specific examples of when and how to set limits will be taught over the next several weeks; you will also have lots of opportunities to practice this very important skill.)

"Be-With" Attitudes:

Your intent in your actions, presence, and responses is what is most important and should convey to your child:

"I am here—I hear you—I understand—I care—I delight in you!"

Goals of the Play Sessions:

1. To allow the child—through the medium of play—to communicate thoughts, needs, and feelings to his parent, and for the parent to communicate that understanding back to the child.
2. To help the child experience more positive feelings of self-respect, self-worth, confidence, and competence—through feeling accepted, understood, and valued—and ultimately develop self-control, responsibility for actions, and learn to get needs met in appropriate ways.
3. To strengthen the parent-child relationship and foster a sense of trust, security, and closeness for both parent and child.
4. To increase the level of playfulness and enjoyment between parent and child. Enjoy 30 minutes of time together!

Child-Parent Relationship Therapy (CPRT)

Session 3—Treatment Outline

⌚ Time Marker

*Note: **See Companion Website** Appendix A to download and print Materials Checklist and any additional materials for this session. Also print **Dos and Don'ts Poster**, Appendix C, and display next to the monitor. The CPRT Training Resources section in this manual provides information about suggested books and videos*

________ **I. Informal Sharing and Review of Homework**

- Parents share toys collected and inexpensive resources.
- Parents share time and place for play sessions

  Important to ask specific questions about when and where
- Hand out appointment cards—one for parent and one for child to keep (Suggest taping card to mirror in bathroom where child brushes teeth)

________ **II. *Play Session Procedures Checklist*** handout: (*Parent Notebook* p. 135)

- Briefly go over handout—especially what to do before the session to structure for success. Ask parents to read over carefully at least 2 days before their play session.
- Refer parents to photograph (p. 137) showing toys set up for play session.

________ **III. *Play Session Dos & Don'ts*** handout: (*Parent Notebook* p. 136); also refer to ***Play Session Dos & Don'ts*** poster

- Begin with brief review of **Don'ts**: Ask parents to circle the **Don't** that will be hardest for them.

  Don't:

  1. Don't criticize any behavior.
  2. Don't praise the child.
  3. Don't ask leading questions.
  4. Don't allow interruptions of the session.
  5. Don't give information or teach.
  6. Don't preach.
  7. Don't initiate new activities.
  8. Don't be passive or quiet.

  (Don'ts 1–7 are taken from Guerney, 1972.)

- Next, ask parents to refer to *Play Session* ***Dos***. Ask them to circle 1, 2, 3, & 6. *Emphasize those are the only* ***Dos*** *parents need to focus on in the first play session.*

Do:

1. **Do set the stage (structuring).**
2. **Do let the child lead.**
3. **Do join in the child's play actively, as a follower.**
4. Do verbally track child's play (describe what you see).
5. Do reflect the child's feelings.
6. **Do set firm and consistent limits** (give two brief examples. e.g. Play-Doh, dart gun).
7. Do salute the child's power and encourage effort.
8. Do be verbally active.

______ **IV. Demonstration of Play Session Dos:** View Video Clip (preferably) and/or Conduct a Live Demonstration

- Video clip should focus on demonstrating the "Be-With" Attitudes and **Dos** 1, 2, & 3; secondary focus on 4 – track child's play/describe what you see
- Briefly review 2 limit setting examples with dart gun and Play Doh if you have not. Focus on Communicate the limit and Target an alternative

______ **V. Parent Partners Role-Play**

Have parents take turns being the parent and practice skills they saw you demonstrate, as well as practice beginning and ending the session.

______ **VI. Discuss with Parents How to Explain "Special Playtime" to Their Child**

Example explanation: "You may wish to explain to your child that you are having these special playtimes with her because *'I am going to this special play class to learn some special ways to play with you!'* "

______ **VII. Arrange for One to Two Parent(s) to Video-Record This Week**

Hint: Handpick the first 1–2 parents whom you think will be most successful

- Name/phone number ____________ day/time (if recording at clinic) ____________
- Name/phone number ____________ day/time (if recording at clinic) ____________
- Remind parent(s) who are video-recording this week to make note on their *Parent Notes and Homework* handout.

______ **VIII. Homework Assignments** (*Parent Notebook* p. 134)

☐ Complete play session toy kit—get blanket/tablecloth and other materials (see *Photograph of Toys Set Up for Play Session* in handouts) and confirm that the time and place you chose will work. Make arrangements for other children.

- ☐ Explain to your child why you are having these special playtimes with him or her. Then, give your child an appointment card (display where child can see the card: suggest taping card to mirror in the bathroom where child brushes teeth).

- ☐ Make "Special Playtime—Do Not Disturb" sign with child 1 to 3 days ahead (depending on child's age). The younger the child, the closer to the time of play session.

  Note to Therapist: Print out *Appointment Cards* and *Template for "Do Not Disturb" Sign* from Appendix A in the Companion Website and distribute to parents.

- ☐ Read handouts prior to play session:
  - *Play Session Procedures Checklist*
  - *Play Session Dos & Don'ts*

- ☐ Play sessions begin at home this week—arrange to video-record your session and make notes about problems or questions you have about your sessions.

____ ***I will bring my video next week (if video-recording at clinic: my appt. day/time ________).***

_______ IX. Close with Motivational Poem, Story, or Rule of Thumb (optional)

RULE OF THUMB TO REMEMBER:

"Be a thermostat, not a thermometer."

Reflecting/responding to your child's thoughts, feelings, and needs creates an atmosphere of understanding and acceptance for your child and helps prevent problems.

CHILD-PARENT-RELATIONSHIP (C-P-R) TRAINING
Parent Notes and Homework—Session 3

RULE OF THUMB TO REMEMBER:

"Be a thermostat, not a thermometer."

Reflecting/responding to your child's thoughts, feelings, and needs creates an atmosphere of understanding and acceptance for your child and helps prevent problems.

During the 30-minute play session, you are to be a thermostat for your child.

Basic Limit Setting:

Focus on Communicate the limit and Target an alternative

If child picks up the gun and aims it at you:

"Jamal, I know you'd like to shoot the gun at me, but I'm not for shooting. You can choose to shoot at that" (point at something acceptable)."

If child starts to smash Play-Doh on the floor:

"Lucy, I know you're really having fun with that, but the Play-Doh is not for the floor/carpet. You can choose to smash it on the tray or a piece of paper."

Notes: (use back for additional notes)

____

____

____

____

Homework Assignments:

- ☐ Complete play session toy kit—get blanket and other materials (see *Photograph of Toys Set Up for Play Session* in handouts) and confirm that the time and place you chose will work. Make arrangements for other children.
- ☐ *Explain to your child that you are having these special playtimes with him or her because "I am going to this special play class to learn some special ways to play with you!"* Then, give your child an appointment card (display where child can see the card: suggest taping card to mirror in the bathroom where child brushes teeth).
- ☐ *Make "Special Playtime—Do Not Disturb" sign with child 1 to 3 days ahead (depending on child's age). The younger the child, the closer to the time of play session.*
- ☐ Read over handouts prior to play session:
  - *Play Session Procedures Checklist*
  - *Play Session Dos & Don'ts*
- ☐ Play sessions begin at home this week—arrange to video-record your session and make notes about problems or questions you have about your sessions.

____ I will bring my video next week (if video-recording at clinic: my appt. day/time ____).

CHILD-PARENT-RELATIONSHIP (C-P-R) TRAINING
Play Session Procedures Checklist—Session 3

Depending on age of child, may need to remind him or her: "Today is the day for our special playtime!"

A. Prior to Session (Remember to "Set the Stage")

- ☐ Make arrangements for other family members (so that there will be no interruptions).
- ☐ Prepare a snack or activity for after the play session (see item D. below)
- ☐ Set up toys on old quilt—keep toy placement predictable.
- ☐ Have a clock visible in the room (or wear a watch).
- ☐ Put pets outside or in another room.
- ☐ Let the child use the bathroom prior to the play session.
- ☐ Switch on video recorder.

B. Beginning the Session

- ☐ Child and Parent: Hang "Do Not Disturb" sign (can also "unplug" phone if there is one in play session area). *Message to child: "This is so important that No One is allowed to interrupt this time together."*
- ☐ Tell Child: "*We will have 30 minutes of special playtime, and you can play with the toys in lots of the ways you want to.*"
  (Voice needs to convey that parent is looking forward to this time with child.)
- ☐ From this point let the child lead.

C. During the Session

- ☐ Sit on the same level as child, close enough to show interest but allowing enough space for child to move freely.
- ☐ Focus your eyes, ears, and body fully on child. (Toes Follow Nose!) Conveys full attention!
- ☐ Your voice should mostly be gentle and caring, but vary with the intensity and affect of child's play.
- ☐ Allow the child to identify the toys. (To promote make-believe play [e.g., what looks like a car to you might be a spaceship to your child], try to use nonspecific words ["this," "that," "it"] if child hasn't named toy.)
- ☐ Play actively with the child, if the child requests your participation.
- ☐ Verbally reflect what you see and hear (child's play/activity, thoughts, feelings).
- ☐ Set limits on behaviors that make you feel uncomfortable.
- ☐ Give 5-minute advance notice for session's end and then a 1-minute notice.
  ("*Anika, we have 5 minutes left in our special playtime.*")

D. Ending the Session

- ☐ At 30 minutes, stand and announce, **"Our playtime is over for today."** Do not exceed time limit by more than 2 to 3 minutes.
- ☐ Parent does the cleaning up. If child chooses, child may help. (If child continues to play while "cleaning," set limit below.)
- ☐ If child has difficulty leaving:
  - Open the door or begin to put away toys.
  - Reflect child's feelings about not wanting to leave, but calmly and firmly restate that the playtime is over. (Restate limit as many times as needed—the goal is for child to be able to stop herself.)
    "I know you would like to stay and play with the toys, but our special playtime is over for today."
  - Adding a statement that gives child something to look forward to helps child see that, although she cannot continue to play with the special toys, there is something else she can do that is also enjoyable. For example:
    1. **"You can play with the toys (or specific toy) next week during our special playtime."**
    2. **"It's time for snack; would you like grapes or cherries today?"**
    3. **"We can go outside and play on the trampoline."**

Note: Patience is the order of the day when helping child to leave—OK to repeat limit calmly several times to allow child to struggle with leaving on her own. (Key is showing empathy and understanding in your voice tone and facial expressions as you state the limit.) Younger children may need more time to "hear" limit and respond.

Never use Special Playtime as a reward or consequence—no matter the child's behavior that day!

CHILD-PARENT-RELATIONSHIP (C-P-R) TRAINING
Play Session Dos & Don'ts—Session 3

Parents: *Your major task is to show genuine and intentional interest in your child's play. You communicate your interest in, and understanding of, your child's thoughts, feelings, and behavior through your words, actions, and undivided focus on your child.*

Do:

1. **Do set the stage. (Structure for Success!)**
    - Prepare play area ahead of time (old blanket can be used to establish a visual boundary of the play area, as well as provide protection for flooring; a cookie sheet under the arts/crafts materials provides a hard surface for Play-Doh, drawing, and gluing and provides ease of clean up).
    - Display the toys in a consistent manner around the perimeter of the play area.
    - Convey *freedom* as you introduce your special playtime to your child: ***"During our special playtime, you can play with the toys in lots of the ways you'd like to."***
    - Allow your child to lead by returning responsibility to your child using responses, such as *"That's up to you," "You can decide,"* or *"That can be whatever you want it to be."*
2. **Do let your child lead.**
    - Allowing your child to lead during the playtime helps you to better understand your child's world and what your child needs from you.
    - Communicate your willingness to follow your child's lead through your responses: *"Show me what you want me to do," "You want me to put that on," "Hmmm . . . ,"* or "I wonder . . ."
    - Use whisper technique (co-conspirators) when child wants you to play a role: *"What should I say?"* or *"What happens next?"* (Modify responses for older kids: use conspiratorial tone, "What happens now?" "What kind of teacher am I?" etc.)
3. **Do join in your child's play actively and playfully, *as a follower*.**
    - Convey your willingness to follow your child's lead through your responses and your actions, by actively joining in the play (child is the director, parent is the actor) using responses such as "So I'm supposed to be the teacher," "You want me to be the robber, and I'm supposed to wear the black mask," "Now I'm supposed to pretend I'm locked up in jail, until you say I can get out," or "You want me to stack these just as high as yours."
    - You can also use the whisper technique described above.
4. **Do verbally track the child's play** (describe what you see).
    - Verbally tracking your child's play is a way of letting your child know that you are paying close attention and that you are interested and involved.
    - Use observational responses, such as *"You're filling that all the way to the top," "You've decided you want to paint next,"* or *"You've got 'em all lined up just how you want them."*
5. **Do reflect your child's feelings.**
    - Verbally reflecting children's feelings helps them feel understood and communicates your acceptance of their feelings and needs.
    - Use reflective responses, such as *"You're proud of your picture," "That kinda surprised you," "You really like how that feels on your hands," "You really wish that we could play longer," "You don't like the way that turned out,"* or *"You sound disappointed." (Hint: Look closely at your child's face to better identify how your child is feeling.)*
6. **Do set firm and consistent limits.**
    - Consistent limits create a structure for a safe and predictable environment for children.
    - Children should never be permitted to hurt themselves or you.
    - Limit setting provides an opportunity for your child to develop self-control and self-responsibility.
    - Using a calm, patient, yet firm voice, say, "I know you're having fun, but *the carpet's not for putting Play-Doh on; you can play with it on the tray"* or *"I know you'd like to shoot the gun at me, but I'm not for shooting. You can choose to shoot at that"* (point to something acceptable).
7. **Do salute the child's power and encourage effort.**
    - Verbally recognizing and encouraging your child's effort builds self-esteem and confidence and promotes self-motivation.
    - Use self-esteem-building responses, such as *"You worked hard on that!" "You did it!" "You figured it out!" "You've got a plan for how you're gonna set those up," "You know just how you want that to be,"* or *"Sounds like you know lots about how to take care of babies."*
8. **Do be verbally active.**
    - Being verbally active communicates to your child that you are interested and involved in her play. If you are silent, your child will feel watched.
    - *Note: Empathic grunts—"Hmm . . ." and so forth—also convey interest and involvement, when you are unsure of how to respond.*

Don't:

1. Don't *criticize* any behavior.
2. Don't praise the child.
3. Don't ask leading questions.
4. Don't allow external interruptions of the session.
5. Don't give information or teach.
6. Don't preach.
7. Don't initiate new activities.
8. Don't be passive or quiet.

(Don'ts 1-7 are taken from Guerney, 1972.)

Remember the "Be-With" Attitudes: Your intent in your responses is what is most important. Convey to your child:

"I am here—I hear you—I understand—I care—I delight in you!"

Reminder: These play session skills (the new skills you are applying) are relatively meaningless if applied mechanically and not as an attempt to be genuinely empathic and truly understand your child. **Your Intent and Attitude Are More Important Than Your Words!**

CHILD-PARENT-RELATIONSHIP (C-P-R) TRAINING
Photograph of Toys Set Up for Play Session—Session 3

Child-Parent Relationship Therapy (CPRT)

Session 4—Treatment Outline

⌚ Time Marker

Note: ***See Companion Website*** *Appendix A to download and print* ***Materials Checklist*** *and any additional materials for this session. Also print* ***Dos and Don'ts Poster****, Appendix C, and display next to the monitor. The CPRT Training Resources section in this manual provides information about suggested books and videos.*

______ **I. Informal Sharing, followed by Parent Sharing Highlights of Preparing for and Conducting Home Play Sessions** (parents with video go last)

- Be aware of time as parents share how their week has gone—keep group process moving!
- During informal sharing, parents often report times during the week when their children were upset and parents didn't know how to respond. *The following Rule of Thumb can be used when it naturally fits with parents' comments or at the end of the session.*

  Rule of Thumb: When a child is drowning, don't try to teach her to swim.

  When a child is feeling upset or out of control, that is not the moment to impart a rule or teach a lesson.

  Your job is to "save your child" when he/she is drowning in emotions. You can help calm your child and co-regulate his/her feelings and behavior by calmly conveying your understanding and acceptance in your words and actions.
- Transition into parents sharing about their play sessions.
- Model encouragement by prizing parents' efforts.
- Use parents' sharing to emphasize examples of **Play Session Dos**; look for something positive to reflect for <u>each</u> parent.
- Refer to poster or handout and encourage parents' efforts to recognize the **Play Session Dos**.
- Seize opportunities to forge connections between parents with similar struggles.

______ **II. Video-Recorded Play Session Review and Supervision**

Note: *Comment on the* ***positive****, taking a few words the parent said or nonverbal behavior and turning that into a* ***Play Session Do*** *or another teaching point* ***(Remember, the Donut Analogy applies to parents, too)****.*

- Encourage the parent who video-recorded the session to share what it was like to be video-recorded knowing that she would have to share it with the class.
- Ask if the parent has a question about some part of the session or if there is some part he/she would particularly like to show—play that portion of the video. If the parent does not have a spot to start, fast forward approximately 5–8 minutes.

- Play video until a strength is evident.
- Focus on importance of parent's awareness of self in the play session.
- Identify *only one* thing the parent might do differently.
- After stopping the video, refer parents to *Play Session Dos & Don'ts* poster or handout. Ask parents to identify the **Dos** they saw demonstrated in the video-recorded play session.

_______ **III.** ***Limit Setting: A-C-T Before It's Too Late!* and *Limit Setting: A-C-T Practice Worksheet*** handouts: (*Parent Notebook* p. 139)

- Briefly review the A-C-T model—go over importance of consistency. (optional) Show video clip on limit setting.
- Parent is in charge of the structure for the play session: selecting the time and place, establishing necessary limits, and enforcing the limits.
- Child is responsible for choices and decisions, within the limits set by parent during playtimes.
- Briefly give a few examples of possible limits to set during play sessions.
- **Rule of Thumb: "During play sessions, limits are not needed until they are needed!"**
- Review *Limit Setting: A-C-T Practice Worksheet* (*Parent Notebook* p. 140)

  Do at least two or three examples together—discuss the rest next week as completed homework; point out question where parents are asked to write down a limit they think they might need to set for their child.
- Be prepared for discussion regarding parent concerns about guns (used in limit-setting example).

_______ **IV. Demonstration of Play Session Skills and Limit Setting Followed by Role-Play**

- Always allow time for parents to see a demonstration of play session skills (video or live) that you want them to emulate, focusing on those skills they report the most difficulty with.
- After viewing demonstration, ask parents to take turns as a parent and a child and role-play a few scenarios they believe will be most difficult for them, including at least one limit-setting role-play.

_______ **V. CPRT Cliff Notes** handout (p. 142 in *Parent Notebook*)

- Ask parents to review prior to this week's play session as a quick review of helpful responses but not to memorize in a rote manner.

______ VI. Arrange for Two Parents to Video-Record This Week

- Name/phone number ________ day/time (if recording at clinic) ______________
- Name/phone number ________ day/time (if recording at clinic) ______________
- Remind parent(s) who are video-recording this week to make note on their *Parent Notes and Homework* handout.

______ VII. Homework Assignments (*Parent Notebook* p. 138)

☐ Complete *Limit Setting: A-C-T Practice Worksheet.*

☐ Read over handouts prior to play session:

- *Limit Setting: A-C-T Before It's Too Late!*
- *CPRT Cliff Notes*
- *Play Session Procedures Checklist* (from Session 3)
- *Play Session Dos & Don'ts* (from Session 3)

☐ Conduct play session (same time and place):

- Complete *Play Session Notes.*
- Notice one feeling in yourself during your play session this week.

____ ***I will bring my video next week (if video-recording at clinic: my appt. day/time ________).***

______ VIII. Close with Motivational Poem, Story, or Rule of Thumb (optional)

RULES OF THUMB TO REMEMBER:

1. **"When a child is drowning, don't try to teach her to swim."** When a child is feeling upset or out of control, that is not the moment to impart a rule or teach a lesson.

   Your job is to "save your child" when he/she is drowning in emotions. You can help calm your child and co-regulate his/her feelings and behavior by calmly conveying your understanding and acceptance through your words and actions.

   (Optional: Show YouTube video clip of Dan Siegel's "Hand Model of the Brain")

2. **"During play sessions, limits are not needed until they are needed!"**

CHILD-PARENT-RELATIONSHIP (C-P-R) TRAINING
Parent Notes and Homework—Session 4

RULES OF THUMB TO REMEMBER:

1. **"When a child is drowning, don't try to teach her to swim."** When a child is feeling upset or out of control, that is not the moment to impart a rule or teach a lesson.

   Your job is to "save your child" when he/she is drowning in emotions. You can help calm your child and co-regulate his/her feelings and behavior by calmly conveying your understanding and acceptance through your words and actions.
2. **"During play sessions, limits are not needed until they are needed!"**

Basic Limit Setting:

Start by saying child's name: "Sarah,"

Acknowledge the Feeling: *"I know you'd like to shoot the dart gun at me. . . "* (with empathy)

Communicate the Limit: *"but I'm not for shooting."*

Target acceptable Alternative: *You can choose to shoot at that" (point at something acceptable).*

Notes: (use back for additional notes)

____

____

____

____

____

____

Homework Assignments:

- ☐ Complete *Limit Setting: A-C-T Practice Worksheet.*
- ☐ Read over handouts prior to play session:
  - *Limit Setting: A-C-T Before It's Too Late!*
  - *CPRT Cliff Notes*
  - *Play Session Procedures Checklist* (from Session 3)
  - *Play Session Dos & Don'ts* (from Session 3)
- ☐ Conduct play session (same time and place):
  - Complete *Play Session Notes.*
  - Notice one feeling in yourself during your play session this week.

_____ ***I will bring my video next week (if video-recording at clinic: my appt. day/time _____).***

CHILD-PARENT-RELATIONSHIP (C-P-R) TRAINING
Limit Setting: A-C-T Before It's Too Late!—Session 4

Acknowledge the feeling

Communicate the limit

Target alternatives

Three Step A-C-T Method of Limit Setting:

Scenario: Damian has been pretending that the bop bag is a bad guy and shooting him with the dart gun; he looks over at you and aims the dart gun at you, then laughs and says, "Now, you're one of the bad guys, too!"

1. Acknowledge your child's feeling or desire (*your voice must convey empathy and understanding*).
   "Damian, I know that you think that it would be fun to shoot me, too. . . "
   Child learns that his feelings, desires, and wishes are valid and accepted by parent (but not all behavior); just empathically reflecting your child's feeling often defuses the intensity of the feeling or need.
2. Communicate the limit (be specific and clear—and brief).
   "but I'm not for shooting."
3. Target acceptable alternatives (provide one or more choices, depending on age of child).
   "You can pretend that the doll is one of the bad guys (pointing at the doll) and shoot at it."
   The goal is to provide your child with an acceptable outlet for expressing the feeling or the original action, while giving him an opportunity to exercise self-control. Note: Pointing helps redirect child's attention.

When to Set Limits?

✍ **Rule of Thumb: "During play sessions, limits are not needed until they are needed!"**

Limits are set only when the need arises, and for four basic reasons:
- To protect child from hurting himself or parent.
- To protect valuable property.
- To maintain parent's acceptance of child.
- To provide consistency in the play session by limiting child and toys to play area and ending on time.

Before setting a limit in a play session, ask yourself:
- "Is this limit necessary?"
- "Can I consistently enforce this limit?"
- "If I don't' set a limit on this behavior, can I consistently allow this behavior and accept my child?"

Avoid conducting play sessions in areas of the house that require too many limits. Limits set during play sessions should allow for greater freedom of expression than would normally be allowed. The fewer the limits, the easier it is for you to be consistent—**consistency is very important**. Determine a few limits ahead of time (practice A-C-T): no hitting or shooting at parent, no Play-Doh on carpet, no purposefully breaking toys, and so forth. *Hint: Children really do understand that playtimes are "special" and that the rules are different—they will not expect the same level of permissiveness during the rest of the week.*

How to Set Limits?

Limits are not punitive and should be stated firmly, but calmly and matter-of-factly. After empathically acknowledging your child's feeling or desire (very important step), you state, "The Play-Doh is not for throwing at the table," just like you would state, "The sky is blue." Don't try to force your child to obey the limit. Remember to provide an acceptable alternative. In this method, it really is up to the child to decide to accept or break the limit; however, **it is your job, as the parent, to consistently enforce the limit**. Remember to be patient. This is a new experience for your child. It may be necessary to repeat the limit 2-3 times to allow your child to bring self under control.

Why Establish Consistent Limits?

Providing children with consistent limits helps them feel safe and secure. This method of limiting children's behavior teaches them self-control and responsibility for their own behavior by allowing them to experience the consequences of their choices and decisions. Limits set in play sessions help children practice self-control and begin to learn to stop themselves in the real world.

CONSISTENT LIMITS → PREDICTABLE, SAFE ENVIRONMENT → SENSE OF SECURITY

CHILD-PARENT-RELATIONSHIP (C-P-R) TRAINING
Limit Setting: A-C-T Practice Worksheet—Session 4

Acknowledge the feeling
Communicate the limit
Target alternatives

EXAMPLE # 1

Gabrielle is using glue to make a creation during playtime. In attempt to be funny, she puts the glue bottle over your head as if she will squeeze glue in your hair.

A **"Gabrielle, I know that you think that would be funny,"**

C **"but my hair is not for glue."**

T **"You can squeeze glue *all* over on the paper."** (Your voice can match her playfulness.)

EXAMPLE # 2

The play session time is up, and you have stated the limit two times. Your child becomes angry because you won't give in and let him play longer; he begins to hit you. Hitting is not allowed, so go immediately to second step of A-C-T, then follow with all three steps of A-C-T method of limit setting.

C (firmly) **"Eduardo, I'm not for hitting."**

A (empathically) **"I know you're mad/frustrated,"**

C (firmly) **"but people aren't for hitting."**

T (neutral tone) **"You can hit the bop bag or hit this pillow."** (pointing to bop bag or pillow)

PRACTICE:

1. In the midst of a playful sword fight between you and your child, your child hits your face with the foam sword.

   A *[Child's name], I know you're getting excited* .

   C *But my face is not for hitting* .

   T *You can choose to hit my sword or hit at that* (point to bop bag) .

2. After 15 minutes of the play session, your child announces that she wants to leave and go upstairs to play a video game.

   A I know you *would like to go play your game right now* .

   C *but we have 15 minutes more in our special playtime* .

   T Then you can play your game .

Child-Parent-Relationship (C-P-R) Training
Page 2—Limit Setting: A-C-T Practice Worksheet—Session 4

3. Your child wants to play doctor and asks you to be the patient. Your child asks you to pull up your shirt so that she/he can listen to your heart.

   A *[Child's name], I know you want me to pull up my shirt like at a real doctor's office*.

   C *But my shirt is not for pulling up* ______.

   T *You can listen to my heart through my shirt (as you state the alternative, take the stethoscope and place it where you are comfortable)* ______.

4. Describe a situation in which you think you might need to set a limit during the play session.

   Situation: ______________________________

   ____

   A ______________________________

   C ______________________________

   T ______________________________

CHILD-PARENT-RELATIONSHIP (C-P-R) TRAINING
Cliff Notes for Parents—Session 4

Remember:

1. Essential "Be-With" Attitudes: I'm here—I hear you—I understand—I care—I delight in you!
2. Importance of nonverbals (face and voice congruent with words; toes follow nose; lean towards child)
3. Avoid asking questions; instead make reflections/statements (trust your experience/instinct; sometimes you aren't sure, but child will correct you if you are wrong)
4. Often helpful to start reflection with: ***"You/You're. . ."*** to give child credit for actions/intent
5. Other reflections that can be useful in conveying (a) acceptance of the child, (b) freedom of the playtime, (c) belief that the child will take her play in the direction she needs, (d) belief that the child is inherently worthy of being valued and prized, and (e) capable of self-direction and problem solving:

"You're wondering . . ."
"In here, you can decide."
"It can be whatever you want it to be."
"That's up to you."
"Hmm - I wonder. . . . "
"Show me what you want me to do."
"What should I say/do; What happens next?"
(stage whisper - child is director and you are the actor, with no script)
"You know just what you want to do."
"You decided to. . ."
"You did it" (important that your affect matches child)
"You got that just the way you wanted it to go."
"You figured that out."
"You're working hard to get that off."
"You're determined to figure that out."
"You look happy, proud, sad, etc . . . about that."

6. Therapeutic Limit Setting: conveys <u>your empathic understanding of the child's intent/desire</u> and provides the child with the opportunity to bring self under control. **Remember: A-C-T**

   *"Isabella, **(A)** I know you'd like to shoot the picture, **(C)** but, the picture isn't for shooting. **(T)** You can shoot the dart at the wall (pointing to wall)"*

   *"Isabella, **(A)** You'd like to play with the playdoh on the carpet, **(C)** but the playdoh is for staying on the tray" (sometimes you don't need a "T")*

   *"Isabella, **(A)** You'd really like to play longer, but **(C)** our time is up for today. **(T)** We can go outside and play on the trampoline **OR** We can go to the kitchen and get a snack"* (have options prepared ahead of time that you know your child would look forward to)

CHILD-PARENT-RELATIONSHIP (C-P-R) TRAINING
Play Session Notes—Session 4

Play Session # ____________ Date: ____________

Significant Happenings:

What I Learned About My Child:

Feelings Expressed:

Play Themes:

What I Learned About Myself:

My feelings during the play session:

What I think I was best at:

What was hardest or most challenging for me:

Questions or Concerns:

Skill I Want to Focus on in the Next Play Session: ______________________________

Child-Parent Relationship Therapy (CPRT)

Session 5—Treatment Outline

Time Marker

Note: ***See Companion Website*** *Appendix A to download and print* ***Materials Checklist*** *and any additional materials for this session. Display* ***Dos and Don'ts Poster*** *next to the monitor. The CPRT Training Resources section in this manual provides information about suggested books and videos.*

________ **I. Informal Sharing, followed by Review of Homework and Play Session Reports**

(video-recorded parents share last)

- Parents share a feeling they were aware of during their play sessions.

  Focus on importance of parents' self-awareness of their feelings in the play session; Therapist models by reflecting parents' feelings.

- Parents share limit-setting attempts <u>during</u> play sessions. Let parents know you will be reviewing limit-setting homework later in the session.

  Remember to focus only on play session happenings. Parents are often eager to discuss discipline struggles in daily life. Reflect parents' urgency in wanting to discuss limit setting and assure parents that setting limits outside of playtimes will be covered in a few sessions.

- Focus on **Play Session Dos** (Display **Poster** for parents to refer to).

  Use examples from parents' comments to reinforce **Dos**—Point out difficult situations and spontaneously role-play with parents on how to respond.

- **Remember the donut analogy: Focus on strengths and positive examples.**

  Find something in <u>each</u> parent's sharing that can be encouraged and supported—facilitate "connecting" among group members; help them see they are not alone in their struggle to apply these new skills.

________ **II. Video-Recorded Play Session Review and Supervision**

- View two parent-child play sessions, following same procedure as last week: Focus on strengths, model encouragement, and facilitate peer feedback.
- Refer parents to handout, *Play Session Skills Checklist*, in the *Parent Notebook* p. 147, and ask parents to check off skills they see being demonstrated.
- Encourage the parent who video-recorded to share a bit about the play session before starting video.
- Play portion of video that parent has a question about or would particularly like to show. If the parent does not have a preference, fast forward approximately 5–8 minutes.

- Play video until a strength is evident.
- Identify only one thing the parent might do differently.
- After stopping video, refer parents to *Play Session Dos & Don'ts* poster or handout from Session 3 and ask parents to identify Dos they saw demonstrated.
- Focus on importance of parent's awareness of self in the play session.
  - Ask what the parent thinks he/she does well.
  - Ask what area the parent would like to work on in his/her next play session.

_______ **III. Limit-Setting Review**

(Optional) Show video clip on limit setting.

- Review A-C-T Method *Limit Setting: A-C-T Before It's Too Late! (Parent Notebook* p. 139).

  Emphasize importance of using all three steps.

  Emphasize the importance of stating clear and concise limits.

- Review *Limit Setting: A-C-T Practice Worksheet (Parent Notebook* p. 140).

  Go over any scenarios not covered in Session 4 or brought up during review of homework.

  Discuss limits parents thought they might need to set and help use A-C-T to respond.

- Review handout: *Limit Setting: Why Use the Three-Step A-C-T Method? (Parent Notebook* p. 145).

  Ask parents what they think the message to the child might be for each example.

  If not enough time, ask parents to read over at home.

_______ **IV. Demonstration of Play Session Skills and Limit Setting Followed by Role-Play**

- Always allow time for parents to see a demonstration of play session skills (video or live) that you want them to emulate, focusing on those skills they find most difficult.
- After viewing demonstration, ask parents to take turns being the child and parent and role-play a few scenarios they believe are most difficult for them, including at least one limit-setting role-play.

_______ **V. Arrange for Two Parents to Video-Record This Week**

- Name/phone number ___________ day/time (if recording at clinic) ___________
- Name/phone number ___________ day/time (if recording at clinic) ___________
- Remind parent(s) who are video-recording this week to make note on their *Parent Notes and Homework* handout.

______ **VI. Homework Assignments** (*Parent Notebook* p. 144)

☐ Give each of your children a Sandwich Hug and Sandwich Kiss (therapist explains/demonstrates).

☐ Read over handouts prior to play session:

- *Limit Setting: A-C-T Before It's Too Late!* (from Session 4)
- *Play Session Dos & Don'ts* (from Session 3)
- *Play Session Procedures Checklist* (from Session 3)
- CPRT Cliff Notes (from Session 4)

☐ Conduct play session (same time and place):

- Complete *Play Session Notes.*
- Note what you thought you did well, and select one skill you want to work on in your next play session.
- If you needed to set a limit during your playtime, describe what happened and what you said or did.

☐ Additional Assignment:

____ ***I will bring my video next week (if video-recording at clinic: my appt. day/time ________).***

______ **VII. Close with Rule of Thumb or Motivational Story of Poem**

RULE OF THUMB TO REMEMBER:

"If you can't say it in 10 words or less, don't say it."

As parents, we have a tendency to over-explain to our children, and our message gets lost in the words.

When unsure of what to say to your child or what to do, ask yourself, "What action or words will most preserve the relationship or do least harm?" In moments when no one will win or you will damage the relationship, walking away and saying nothing, or telling your child, "I need to take a time-out to cool off, and then we can talk," is best.

Always remember: "Nothing at this moment is more important than my relationship with my child." (Also applies to spouses, significant others, etc.)

CHILD-PARENT-RELATIONSHIP (C-P-R) TRAINING
Parent Notes and Homework—Session 5

RULE OF THUMB TO REMEMBER:

1. **"If you can't say it in 10 words or less, don't say it."** As parents, we have a tendency to over-explain to our children, and our message gets lost in the words.
2. **Nothing at this moment is more important than my relationship with my child.** When unsure of what to say to your child or what to do, ask yourself, "What action or words will most preserve the relationship or do least harm?" In moments when no one will win or you will damage the relationship, walking away and saying nothing, or telling your child, "I need to take a time-out to cool off, and then we can talk," is best.

Notes: (use back for additional notes)

____

____

____

____

____

____

____

Homework Assignments:

- ☐ Give each of your children a Sandwich Hug and Sandwich Kiss.
- ☐ Read over handouts prior to play session:
  - *Limit Setting: A-C-T Before It's Too Late!* (from Session 4)
  - *Play Session Dos & Don'ts* (from Session 3)
  - *Play Session Procedures Checklist* (from Session 3)
  - *CPRT Cliff Notes* (from Session 4)
- ☐ Conduct play session (same time and place):
  - Complete *Play Session Notes.*
  - Note what you thought you did well, and select one skill you want to work on in your next play session.
  - If you needed to set a limit during your playtime, describe what happened and what you said or did.
- ☐ Additional Assignment:

  ____ ***I will bring my video next week (if video-recording at clinic: my appt. day/time ______).***

CHILD-PARENT-RELATIONSHIP (C-P-R) TRAINING
Limit Setting: Why Use the Three-Step A-C-T Method?—Session 5

Acknowledge the feeling

Communicate the limit

Target alternatives

Discuss the different messages that are implied in the following typical parent responses to unacceptable behavior:

- It's probably not a good idea to paint the wall.
  Message: I'm really not sure whether it's okay to paint the wall. It might be okay, or it might not.
- You can't paint the walls in here.
  Message: You might be able to paint the walls in the other room.
- I can't let you paint the wall.
  Message: What you do is my responsibility and not your responsibility.
- Maybe you could paint something else other than the wall.
  Message: Maybe you can paint the furniture.
- The rule is you can't paint the wall.
  Message: How you feel about it doesn't matter.
- The wall is not for painting on.
  Message: You're not bad for wanting to, it's just not for anyone to paint on.

CHILD-PARENT-RELATIONSHIP (C-P-R) TRAINING
Play Session Notes—Session 5

Play Session # __________ Date: ________________

Significant Happenings:

What I Learned About My Child:

Feelings Expressed:

Play Themes:

What I Learned About Myself:

My feelings during the play session:

What I think I was best at:

What was hardest or most challenging for me:

Questions or Concerns:

Skill I Want to Focus on in the Next Play Session: ________________________________

CHILD-PARENT-RELATIONSHIP (C-P-R) TRAINING
Play Session Skills Checklist
For In-Class Review of Video-Recorded Play Session—Session 5

Play Session # ________Date: _______________

(Note: Indicate ✓ in column if skill was used.)

✓	Skill	Notes/Comments
	Set the Stage/Structured Play Session	
	Conveyed "Be-With" Attitudes Full attention/interested Toes followed nose	
	Allowed Child to Lead Avoided giving suggestions Avoided asking questions Returned responsibility to child	
	Followed Child's Lead Physically on child's level Moved closer when child was involved in play Joined in play when invited	
	Reflective Responding Skills:	
	Reflected child's nonverbal play (Tracking)	
	Reflected child's verbalizations (Content)	
	Reflected child's feelings/wants/wishes	
	Voice tone matched child's intensity/affect	
	Responses were brief and interactive	
	Facial expressions matched child's affect	
	Use of Encouragement/Self-Esteem-Building Responses	
	Set Limits, As Needed, Using A-C-T	

Child-Parent Relationship Therapy (CPRT)

Session 6—Treatment Outline

⏲ Time Marker

Note: ***See Companion Website*** *Appendix A to download and print* ***Materials Checklist*** *and any additional materials for this session. Display* ***Dos and Don'ts Poster*** *next to the monitor. The CPRT Training Resources section in this manual provides information about suggested books and videos.*

_______ **I. Informal Sharing, followed by Review of Homework and Play Session Reports** (video-recorded parents share last)

- Parents share experience giving each of their children a Sandwich Hug and Sandwich Kiss.
- Parents share limit-setting attempts during play sessions. Review *A-C-T Limit Setting* as needed (*Parent Notebook* p. 139).

  Remember to focus only on play session happenings—redirect other questions about limit setting by assuring parents that you will be focusing on limit setting outside of play session in a few weeks.

- Parents who did not video this week briefly report on play sessions. Focus on parents' perceived changes in their own behavior.

  Focus on **Play Session Dos** (Display **Poster** for parents to refer to).

  Use examples from parents' comments to reinforce **Dos**.

  Respond to difficult situations and spontaneously role-play with parents on how to respond.

- **Remember the donut analogy: Focus on the positive!** Find something in <u>each</u> parent's sharing that can be encouraged and supported—facilitate "connecting" among group members.

_______ **II. Video-Recorded Play Session Review and Supervision**

- View two parent-child play sessions, following same procedure as last week. Play video until a <u>strength</u> is evident.
- Model encouragement and facilitate peer feedback.
- Refer parents to *Play Session Skills Checklist*, in the *Parent Notebook* pg. ___, and ask parents to check off skills they see being demonstrated.
- When you stop video to give feedback, refer parents to *Play Session Dos & Don'ts* poster. Ask parents to identify **Dos** they saw demonstrated.

  When processing playtime happenings, parents often express concerns about children's play during special playtime and worry that their child will think the behavior is okay outside of playtime, e.g. hitting the baby doll with a hard object and worrying that the child will think it is okay to hit a younger sibling in real life.

Rule of Thumb: "Grant in fantasy what you cannot grant in reality."
In a play session, it is okay to act out feelings and wishes that in reality may require limits.

_______ III. Choice Giving

- Review *Choice Giving 101: Teaching Responsibility & Decision Making* handout (*Parent Notebook* p. 149).

  Providing children with *age-appropriate* choices empowers children. Provide choices *equally* acceptable to the child and to you. Discuss differences between empowering choices and choices used as a consequence.

  Presenting children with choices provides opportunity for decision making and problem solving.

  Providing choices reduces power struggles.

  Rule of Thumb: "Big choices for big kids, little choices for little kids."
  Choices given must be commensurate with child's developmental stage.

- Show video: *Choices, Cookies, & Kids* (suggest showing 15–20 minutes and finish video in Session 7).

- As time allows, review *Advanced Choice Giving: Providing Choices as Consequences* (*Parent Notebook* p. 150).

  Note: This handout can be deferred to Session 7, or partially covered in this session and completed in Session 7.

_______ IV. Demonstration of Play Session Skills and Choice Giving, followed by Role-Play of play session skills

- Always allow time for parents to see a demonstration of play session skills that you want them to emulate, focusing on those skills they report the most difficulty with.

- After viewing demonstration, ask parents to role-play a few scenarios they believe are most difficult for them, including at least one choice-giving role-play.

_______ V. Arrange for Two Parents to Video-Record This Week

- Name/phone number ________ day/time (if recording at clinic) _________________

- Name/phone number ________ day/time (if recording at clinic) _________________

- Remind parent(s) who are video-recording this week to make note on their *Parent Notes and Homework* handout.

_______ VI. Homework Assignments (*Parent Notebook* p. 148)

☐ Read *Choice Giving 101: Teaching Responsibility & Decision Making* and *Advanced Choice Giving: Providing Choices as Consequences.*

- ☐ Read *Common Questions Parents Ask* and mark the top two to three issues you have questions about or write in an issue you are challenged by that is not on the handout.
- ☐ Practice giving an empowering choice (A) outside of the play session. If the opportunity arises, you may also want to try giving a choice as a consequence (B), but not when your child is dysregulated/out of control.

A) Provide choices for the sole purpose of <u>empowering your child</u> (two positive choices for child, where either choice is acceptable to you and either choice is desirable to child).
What happened ____________________
What you said ____________________
How child responded ____________________

B) Practice giving choices as a consequence (where choice giving is used to help your child comply with a necessary action; refer parent to *Oreo Cookie Method* example in *Advanced Choice Giving* handout).
What happened ____________________
What you said ____________________
How child responded ____________________

- ☐ Read over handouts prior to play session:
  - *Limit Setting: A-C-T Before It's Too Late!* (from Session 4)
  - *Play Session Dos & Don'ts* (from Session 3)
  - *Play Session Procedures Checklist* (from Session 3)
  - CPRT Cliff Notes (from Session 4)
- ☐ Conduct play session (same time and place):
  - Complete *Play Session Notes.*
  - Use *Play Session Skills Checklist* to note what you thought you did well, and select one skill you want to work on in your next play session.
  - If you needed to set a limit, describe what happened and what you said or did.
- ☐ Additional Assignment:

____ ***I will bring my video next week (if video-recording at clinic: my appt. day/time ________).***

______ **VII. Close with Motivational Poem, Story, or Rule of Thumb** (optional)

RULES OF THUMB TO REMEMBER:

1. **"Grant in fantasy what you can't grant in reality."** In a play session, it is okay to act out feelings and wishes that in reality may require limits. For example, it's okay for the "baby sister" doll to be thrown out a window in playtime.
2. **"Big choices for big kids, little choices for little kids."** Choices given must be commensurate with child's developmental stage.

CHILD-PARENT-RELATIONSHIP (C-P-R) TRAINING
Parent Notes and Homework—Session 6

RULES OF THUMB TO REMEMBER:

1. **"Grant in fantasy what you can't grant in reality."** In a play session, it is okay to act out feelings and wishes that in reality may require limits. For example, it's okay for the "baby sister" doll to be thrown out a window in playtime.
2. **"Big choices for big kids, little choices for little kids."** Choices given must be commensurate with child's developmental stage.

Notes: (use back for additional notes)

____

____

____

____

____

Homework Assignments:

☐ Read *Choice Giving 101: Teaching Responsibility & Decision Making* and *Advanced Choice Giving: Providing Choices as Consequences.*

☐ Read *Common Questions Parents Ask* and mark the top two to three issues you have questions about or write in an issue you are challenged by that is not on the worksheet.

☐ Practice giving an empowering choice (A) outside of the play session. If the opportunity arises, you may also want to try giving a choice as a consequence (B), but not when your child is dysregulated/out of control.

A) Provide choices for the sole purpose of <u>empowering your child</u> (two positive choices for child, where either choice is acceptable to you and either choice is desirable to child).

What happened ____

What you said ____

How child responded ____

B) Practice giving choices as a consequence (where choice giving is used to help your child comply with a necessary action; see *Oreo Cookie Method* example in *Advanced Choice Giving* handout).

What happened ____

What you said ____

How child responded ____

☐ Read over handouts prior to play session:

- *Limit Setting: A-C-T Before It's Too Late!* (from Session 4)
- *Play Session Dos & Don'ts* (from Session 3)
- *Play Session Procedures Checklist* (from Session 3)
- CPRT Cliff Notes (from Session 4)

☐ Conduct play session (same time and place):

- Complete *Play Session Notes.*
- Note what you thought you did well, and select one skill you want to work on in your next play session.
- If you needed to set a limit, describe what happened and what you said or did.

☐ Additional Assignment:

_____ *I will bring my video next week (if video-recording at clinic: my appt. day/time _____).*

CHILD-PARENT-RELATIONSHIP (C-P-R) TRAINING

Choice Giving 101: Teaching Responsibility & Decision Making—Session 6

- **Providing children with age-appropriate choices empowers children** by allowing them a measure of control over their circumstances.
  - Children who feel more empowered and "in control" are more capable of regulating their own behavior, a prerequisite for self-control.
  - Choices require that children tap into their inner resources, rather than relying on parents (external resources) to stop their behavior or solve the problem for them.
  - If parents always intervene, the child learns that "Mom or Dad will stop me if I get out of hand" or "Mom or Dad will figure out a solution if I get in a jam."
- **Presenting children with choices provides opportunities for decision making and problem solving**.
  - Through practice with choice making, children learn to accept responsibility for their choices and actions and learn they are competent and capable.
  - Choice giving facilitates the development of the child's conscience; as children are allowed to learn from their mistakes, they learn to weigh decisions based on possible consequences.
- **Providing children with choices reduces power struggles** between parent and child and, importantly, preserves the child-parent relationship.
  - Both parent and child are empowered. Parent is responsible for, or in control of, providing parameters for choices. Children are responsible for, or in control of, their decision (within parent-determined parameters).

Choice-Giving Strategies

- **Provide age-appropriate choices** that are equally acceptable to the child and to you (parent). Remember that you must be willing to live with the choice the child makes.
- Don't use choices to try and manipulate the child to do what you want by presenting one choice that you want the child to choose and a second choice that you know the child won't like.
- **Provide little choices to little kids; big choices to big kids**. *Example: A 3-year-old can only handle choosing between two shirts or two food items.* ***"Sasha, do you want to wear your red dress or your pink dress to school?" "Sasha, do you want an apple or orange with your lunch?"***

Choice Giving to Avoid Potential Problem Behavior and Power Struggles

- Choices can be used *to avoid a potential problem*. Similar to the example above, choices given are equally acceptable to parent and child. In this case, choices are planned in advance by the parent to avoid problems that the child has a history of struggling with. In the example above, if Sasha has trouble getting dressed in the morning, provide a choice of what to wear the evening before (to avoid a struggle the next morning); after she has made the choice, take the dress out of the closet, ready for morning.
- Children who are given the responsibility for making a decision are more likely to abide by the decision.
- In selecting choices to prevent problems, it is very important that parents understand the real problem that their child is struggling with and plan ahead to prevent the problem.
  - If your child always comes home hungry and wants something sweet, but you want him to have a healthy snack, plan ahead by having on hand at least two choices of healthy snacks that your child likes. Before he heads for the ice cream, say:

    "Antonia, I bought grapes and cherries for snack; which would you like?"
  - If you know your 9-year-old child tends to head straight for the couch to watch TV after school, plan ahead to brainstorm alternative options for your child to do after school.

    "Ana, I thought of some things we can do this afternoon before dinner. Do you want to go outside and play catch or help bake a cake for dessert tonight?"

Hint: This is another place where "structuring for success" can be applied by eliminating the majority of unacceptable snack items, instead stocking up on healthy snack items, and having acceptable activities planned when children arrive home. Structuring your home environment to minimize conflict allows both you and your child to feel more "in control." Remember: **Be a thermostat!**

CHILD-PARENT-RELATIONSHIP (C-P-R) TRAINING

Advanced Choice Giving: Providing Choices as Consequences—Sessions 6-7

Children need parental guidance and discipline. In many instances, parents must make decisions for children—decisions that children are not mature enough to take responsibility for—such as bedtime, other matters of health and safety, and compliance with household policies and rules. However, parents can provide their children with some measure of control in the situation by providing choices. Parents are reminded of the importance of connecting with their child and being sensitive to their emotional state when giving choices or limiting behavior. Remember the Rule of Thumb: "When a child is drowning, don't try to teach her to swim." When children are feeling upset or out of control, they have difficulty hearing choices and consequences. First connect and help calm your child (co-regulate through reflecting child's feelings in soothing voice), then provide choice or wait until a later time.

Oreo® Cookie Method of Choice Giving (from *Choices, Cookies, & Kids* video by Dr. Garry Landreth)

Example 1: Three-year-old Isabella is clutching a handful of Oreo® cookies, ready to eat them all (it is right before bedtime, and the parent knows it would not be healthy for Isabella to have all the cookies. But Isabella does not know that—she just knows that she wants cookies!): **"Isabella, you can choose to keep one of the cookies to eat and put the rest back, or you can put all of the cookies back—which do you choose?"** Or, if it is permissible to the parent for Isabella to have two cookies: **"Isabella, you can have one cookie or two—which do you choose?"**

Example 2: Six-year-old Oliver does not want to take his medicine and adamantly tells you so! Taking the medicine is not a choice—that is a given. But the parent can provide the child with some choice in the situation by saying, **"Oliver, you can choose to have apple juice or orange juice with your medicine—which do you choose?"**

Example 3: Eight-year-old Omar is tired and cranky and refuses to get in the car to go home from Grandma and Grandpa's house. **"Omar, you can choose to sit in the middle row by Daddy, or you can choose to sit in the back seat with Selin—which do you choose?"**

Choice Giving to Enforce Household Policies and Rules

Choice giving can be used to enforce household policies/rules. Begin by working on one at a time. In general, provide two choices—one is phrased positively (consequence for complying with policy), and the other choice (consequence for not complying with policy) is stated as a consequence that you believe your child would not prefer (such as giving up favorite TV show). Consequence for non-compliance should be relevant and logical rather than punitive, and it must be **enforceable**.

Example: A household rule has been established that toys in the family room must be picked up off the floor before dinner (children cannot seem to remember without being told repeatedly, and parent is feeling frustrated with constant reminders and power struggles).

"We are about to institute a new and significant policy within the confines of this domicile" (big words get children's attention!). **"When you choose to pick up your toys before dinner, you choose to watch 30 minutes of television after dinner. When you choose not to pick up your toys before dinner, you choose not to watch television after dinner."** *Note: Be sure to let children know when there are 10–15 minutes before dinner, so they have time to pick up their toys.*

Children may be unable to comply the first time you announce this new policy, because you have just informed them. But what is important is that you begin to allow your children to use their internal resources and self-control to remember the new policy without constant reminders. (Remember that the new policy was implemented because you were frustrated and tired of nagging!) So, the second night, parent says, **"Joaquin and Jamal, dinner will be ready in 10 minutes; it is time to pick up your toys."** Parent walks out. When it is time for dinner, parent goes back into room to announce dinner:

a. The toys have not been picked up—say nothing at that moment. After dinner, go back into family room and announce to children, **"Looks like you decided to not watch television tonight."** Even if children get busy picking up the toys, they have already chosen not to watch TV for this night. **"Oh, you're thinking that if you pick your toys up now that you can watch TV, but the policy is that toys have to be put away before dinner."** After children plead for another chance, *follow through on the consequence*, calmly and empathically stating: **"I know that you wish you would have chosen to put your toys away before dinner, so you could choose to watch TV now. Tomorrow night, you can choose to put your toys away before dinner and choose to watch TV."** *Some children will choose not to watch TV for several nights in a row!*
b. The children are busy picking up toys and have put most of them away. Parent says (as she helps with the few remaining toys to demonstrate spirit of cooperation and prevent delay of dinner), **"It's time for dinner—looks like you've chosen to watch TV after dinner tonight."**

Guidelines for Choice Giving in Relation to Limit Setting and Consequences

- Enforce consequence **without fail** and **without anger.**
- Consequence is for "today" only—***each day (or play session) should be a chance for a fresh start; a chance to have learned from the previous decision and resulting consequence; a chance to use internal resources to control "self" and make a different decision.***
- **Reflect** child's choice with empathy, but remain firm. Consistency and follow-through are critical!
- **Communicate** choices in a matter-of-fact voice—power struggles are likely to result if child hears frustration or anger in parent's voice and believes parent is invested in one choice over another. Child must be free to choose consequence for noncompliance.

Caution: *Once your child has reached the stage of "out of control," your child may not be able to hear and process a choice. Take a step back and focus on your child's feelings, reflecting their feelings empathically while limiting unacceptable behavior.*

Remember the oxygen mask analogy: You (parent) must remain calm and relational during choice giving/limit setting in order for child to perceive that they do have a genuine choice in the situation and avoid power struggle. Parent remains calm, neutral, and relational. You want your child to be successful in choosing!

CHILD-PARENT-RELATIONSHIP (C-P-R) TRAINING

Common Questions Parents Ask—Session 6

Q: My child notices that I talk differently in the play sessions and wants me to talk normally. What should I do?

A: Say, "I sound different to you. That's my way of letting you know I heard what you said. Remember, I'm going to that special class to learn how to play with you." (The child may be saying he notices the parent is different; having a surprise reaction to the verbal attention; annoyed by too much reflection of words; or saying he notices the difference in the parent's reflective-type responses. The child may also be saying he doesn't want the parent to change, because that will mean he must then change and adjust to the parent's new way of responding.)

Q: My child asks many questions during the play sessions and resents my not answering them. What should I do?

A: We always begin by reflecting the child's feelings. "You're angry at me." Sometimes a child feels insecure when a parent changes typical ways of responding and is angry because he doesn't know how to react. Your child may feel insecure and be trying to get your attention the way he has done in the past. Your objective is to encourage your child's self-reliance and self-acceptance. "In our special playtime, the answer can be anything you want it to be." For example, your child might ask, "What should I draw?" You want your child to know he's in charge of his drawing during the special playtime, so you respond, "You've decided to draw, and in this special playtime, you can draw whatever you decide." Our objective is to empower the child, to enable the child to discover his own strengths.

Q: My child just plays and has fun. What am I doing wrong?

A: Nothing. Your child is supposed to use the time however she wants. The relationship you are building with your child during the special playtimes is more important than whether or not your child is working on a problem. As your relationship with your child is strengthened, your child's problem will diminish. Your child may be working on issues through her play that you are not aware of. Remember the lesson of the bandage. What you are doing in the playtimes is working, even when you don't see any change. Children can change as a result of what they do in play sessions with parents or play therapists, even though we are not aware of what they are working on. Your job during the special playtimes is to follow your child's lead and be nonjudgmental, understanding, and accepting of your child. Your empathic responses will help your child focus on the issues that are important to her.

Q: I'm bored. What's the value of this?

A: Being bored in a playtime is not an unusual happening because parents have busy schedules, are on the go a lot, and are not used to sitting and interacting quietly for 30 minutes. You can increase your interest level and involvement in your child's play by responding to what you see in your child's face and asking yourself questions such as "What is he feeling?" "What is he trying to say in his play?" "What does he need from me?" or "What is so interesting to him about the toy or the play?" and by making more tracking responses and reflective responses. The most important thing you can do is continue to be patient with the process of the play sessions.

Q: My child doesn't respond to my comments. How do I know I'm on target?

A: Usually when you are on target, your child will let you know. If she doesn't respond to a reflection, you may want to explore other feelings she might be having or convey that you're trying to understand. For example, if you have reflected "You really are angry!" and your child doesn't respond, you might say, "Or maybe it's not anger you're feeling, maybe you're just feeling really strong and powerful." If your child still doesn't respond, you might say, "Maybe that's not it either. I wonder what it could be that you're feeling."

Q: When is it okay for me to ask questions, and when is it not okay?

A: Most of the time, questions can be rephrased as statements, for example, "I wonder if that's ever happened to you" instead of "Has that ever happened to you?" The only type of questions that are okay in play sessions are spoken as "stage whispers," as in "What should I say?"

Q: My child hates the play sessions. Should I discontinue them?

A: Communicating understanding is always important. Say, "You don't want to have the special playtime. You would rather do something else. Let's have the special playtime for 10 minutes, then you can decide if you want to have the rest of the special playtime or do something else." This response helps your child to feel understood and to feel in control. A child in that position in a relationship is much more likely to compromise. In most cases, a child will get started playing and will decide to have the rest of the playtime.

Q: My child wants the playtime to be longer. Should I extend the session?

A: Even though your child is having lots of fun, the time limit is adhered to because this promotes consistency, affords you an opportunity to be firm, and provides your child with an opportunity to bring himself under control and end a very desirable playtime. Use A-C-T limit setting, being sure to acknowledge your child's feelings. For example, you can say, "You're really having fun and would like to play a lot longer, but our special playtime is over for today. We will have another special playtime next Tuesday." If your child persists, you could say, "Joey, I wish we had more time, too, but our 30 minutes are up for today. We'll get to have another playtime next Tuesday."

Q: My child wants to play with the toys at other times during the week. Is that OK?

A: Allowing your child to play with these toys only during the 30-minute playtimes helps to convey the message that this is a special time, a time just for the two of you, a fun time. Setting the toys apart makes the playtime unique and more desirable. Another reason is that this time with your child is an emotional relationship time; the toys become a part of that emotional relationship during which your child expresses and explores emotional messages through the toys because of the kinds of empathic responses you make. This same kind of emotional exploration cannot occur during other playtimes because you are not there to communicate understanding of your child's play. Additionally, being allowed to play with these toys only during the special playtimes helps your child learn to delay his need for gratification. If you are having trouble keeping your child from playing with the special toy kit, try storing it out of sight on the top shelf of your closet. If that doesn't work, lock it in the trunk of your car.

Q: My child wants me to shoot at him during the play session. What should I do?

A: Set the limit. If your child says, "I'm the bad guy, shoot me," say, "I know you want me to shoot you, but you're not for shooting; I can pretend you're the bad guy getting away, and I'll catch you, or you can draw a picture of the bad guy getting shot."

Q: ____

____

____

____

CHILD-PARENT-RELATIONSHIP (C-P-R) TRAINING
Play Session Notes—Session 6

Play Session # ________ Date: ________________

Significant Happenings:

What I Learned About My Child:

Feelings Expressed:

Play Themes:

What I Learned About Myself:

My feelings during the play session:

What I think I was best at:

What was hardest or most challenging for me:

Questions or Concerns:

Skill I Want to Focus on in the Next Play Session: ________________________________

CHILD-PARENT-RELATIONSHIP (C-P-R) TRAINING

Play Session Skills Checklist

For In-Class Review of Video-Recorded Play Session—Session 6

Play Session # ________ Date: ______________

(Note: Indicate ✓ in column if skill was used.)

✓	Skill	Notes/Comments
	Set the Stage/Structured Play Session	
	Conveyed "Be-With" Attitudes Full attention/interested Toes followed nose	
	Allowed Child to Lead Avoided giving suggestions Avoided asking questions Returned responsibility to child	
	Followed Child's Lead Physically on child's level Moved closer when child was involved in play Joined in play when invited	
	Reflective Responding Skills:	
	Reflected child's nonverbal play (Tracking)	
	Reflected child's verbalizations (Content)	
	Reflected child's feelings/wants/wishes	
	Voice tone matched child's intensity/affect	
	Responses were brief and interactive	
	Facial expressions matched child's affect	
	Use of Encouragement/Self-Esteem-Building Responses	
	Set Limits, As Needed, Using A-C-T	

Child-Parent Relationship Therapy (CPRT)

Session 7—Treatment Outline

⌚ Time Marker

Note: ***See Companion Website*** *Appendix A to download and print* ***Materials Checklist*** *and any additional materials for this session. Display* ***Dos and Don'ts Poster*** *next to the monitor. The CPRT Training Resources section in this manual provides information about suggested books and videos.*

_______ **I. Informal Sharing, followed by Review of Homework and Play Session Reports**
(video-recorded parents share last)

- Review *Choice Giving 101: Teaching Responsibility & Decision Making* (*Parent Notebook* p. 149).

  Reinforce basic concepts as parents report on homework assignment to practice giving a choice to their child outside the play session.

- Complete video, *Choices, Cookies, & Kids*, from Session 6.

  Note: Parents may express difficulty in being consistent in disciplining their children and maintaining household rules and routines. Remind parents that, for children:

  Parental consistency > predictability > security > child feeling safe and loved!

- Review and complete as needed: *Advanced Choice Giving: Providing Choices as Consequences* (*Parent Notebook* p. 150).

  If parents raise questions about how choices can be used when the child doesn't comply with a limit, briefly discuss the use of choices as consequences. Inform parents that this more advanced skill will be covered in depth in Session 9.

- Briefly review *Common Questions Parents Ask* (*Parent Notebook* p. 152).

  Ask parents their top concerns and any concern not listed.

  Use as an opportunity to review reflective listening, setting limits, giving choices, and so forth.

- Parents who did not video this week briefly report on play sessions, focusing on parents' perceived changes in their own behavior.

  Focus on **Play Session Dos**.

  Use examples from parents' comments to reinforce **Dos**.

  Role-play with parents on how to respond to difficult situations.

  Remember the Donut Analogy: Encourage and Support!

  Find something in <u>each</u> parent's sharing that can be encouraged.

  Facilitate connections among group members.

______ **II. Video-Recorded Play Session Review and Supervision**

- View two parent-child play sessions, following same procedure as last week. Play video until a strength is evident.
- Model encouragement and facilitate peer feedback.
- Refer parents to handout, *Play Session Skills Checklist*, in the *Parent Notebook* p. 155 and ask parents to check off skills they see being demonstrated.
- When you stop video to give feedback, refer parents to Play Session **Dos & Don'ts** poster. Ask parents to identify Dos they saw demonstrated.
- Focus on importance of parent's awareness of self in the play session.
  - Ask what the parent thinks he/she does well.
  - Ask what area the parent would like to work on in his/her next play session.

______ **III. Self-Esteem Building handout: *Esteem-Building Responses***
(*Parent Notebook* p. 157).

- **Rule of Thumb: "Never do for a child that which he can do for himself."**

  When you do, you rob your child of the joy of discovery and the opportunity to feel competent. You will never know what your child is capable of unless you allow him to try!

______ **IV. Demonstration of Play Session Skills and Esteem-Building Responses, followed by Role-Play**

- Always allow time for parents to see a demonstration of play session skills that you want them to emulate, focusing on those skills they report the most difficulty with.
- After viewing demonstration, ask parents to role-play a few scenarios they believe are most difficult for them, including at least one self-esteem-building response in role-play.

______ **V. Arrange for Two Parents to Video-Record This Week**

- Name/phone number __________ day/time (if recording at clinic) ______________
- Name/phone number __________ day/time (if recording at clinic) ______________
- Remind parent(s) who are video-recording this week to make note on their *Parent Notes and Homework* handout.

______ **VI. Homework Assignments** (*Parent Notebook* p. 156)

☐ Read *Esteem-Building Responses*—practice giving at least one esteem-building response during your play session, also practice giving one esteem-building response outside of your play session.

What happened outside of play session ______________________________
What you said ____
How child responded (verbally or nonverbally) ________________________

☐ Write a note to your child of focus, as well as other children in the family, pointing out a positive character quality you appreciate about the child (see *Positive Character Qualities handout*). Write down the following sentence:

"Dear __________, I was just thinking about you, and what I was thinking is you are so _____________ (thoughtful, responsible, considerate, loving, etc.). I love you, ____________ (Mom, Dad)."

Say to the child, in your own words, after the child reads the note (or you read it to the child), "That is such an important quality; we should put that note on the refrigerator (bulletin board, etc.)." **Reminder:** Don't expect a response from your child.

Continue to write a note each week for at least 3 weeks (suggest mailing first note to your child). Be creative in thinking of places you could leave a note for child to find, e.g., put note in lunchbox.

These notes are a way to be intentional in letting your children know that they are special and that you see them and their positive character qualities. You're adding to their self-concept: Your note saying, "You are responsible" internalizes with the child as "I am responsible."

When you observe your child exhibiting a positive character quality, provide genuine feedback. For example, you observe your child sharing her snack with her sibling. You can respond by stating, *"Alexandria, that was thoughtful of you to share your snack with Jeremiah."*

☐ Read over handouts prior to play session:

- *Limit Setting: A-C-T Before It's Too Late!* (from Session 4)
- *Play Session Dos & Don'ts* (from Session 3)
- *Play Session Procedures Checklist* (from Session 3)
- CPRT Cliff Notes (from Session 4)

☐ Conduct play session (same time and place):

- Complete *Play Session Notes.*
- Note what you thought you did well, and select one skill you want to work on in your next play session.
- Note use of esteem building responses.
- If you needed to set a limit, describe what happened and what you said or did.

☐ Additional Assignment:

____ ***I will bring my video next week (if video-recording at clinic: my appt. day/time ____).***

______ **VII. Close with Motivational Poem, Story, or Rule of Thumb** (optional)

Suggest reading: "*The Struggle to Become a Butterfly: A True Story*" (refer parents to handout, *Esteem-Building Responses*, in the *Parent Notebook* p. 157).

Remember the butterfly: **Without the struggle, there are no wings!**

RULE OF THUMB TO REMEMBER:

"Never do for a child that which he can do for himself."

When you do, you rob your child of the joy of discovery and the opportunity to feel competent. You will never know what your child is capable of unless you allow him to try!

CHILD-PARENT-RELATIONSHIP (C-P-R) TRAINING
Parent Notes and Homework—Session 7

RULE OF THUMB TO REMEMBER:

"Never do for a child that which he can do for himself."
When you do, you rob your child of the joy of discovery and the opportunity to feel competent.
You will never know what your child is capable of unless you allow him to try!

Notes: (use back for additional notes)

____

____

____

____

____

____

____

____

Homework Assignments:

☐ Read *Esteem-Building Responses*—practice giving at least one esteem-building response <u>during</u> your play session. Also practice giving one esteem-building response <u>outside</u> of your play session.
What happened outside of play session ____________________
What you said ____________________
How child responded (verbally or nonverbally) ____________________

☐ Write a note to your child of focus, as well as other children in the family, pointing out a positive character quality you appreciate about your child (see *Positive Character Qualities handout*). Write the following sentence:

"Dear ____________, I was just thinking about you, and what I was thinking is you are so ____________ (thoughtful, responsible, considerate, loving, etc.). I love you, ____________ (Mom, Dad)."

- Continue to write a note each week for 3 weeks (mail first note to child, if possible). Be creative in thinking of places you could leave a note for child to find, e.g., put note in lunchbox.
- **Reminder:** Don't expect a response from your child.

These notes are a way to be intentional in letting your child know that they are special and you *see* them and their positive qualities. You're adding to their self-concept: Your note saying, "You are responsible" internalizes with the child as "I am responsible."

When you observe your child exhibiting a positive character quality, provide genuine feedback. For example, you observe your child sharing her snack with her sibling. You can respond by stating, "*Alexandria, that was thoughtful of you to share your snack with Jeremiah.*"

☐ Read over handouts prior to play session:

- *Limit Setting: A-C-T Before It's Too Late!* (from Session 4)
- *Play Session Dos & Don'ts* (from Session 3)
- *Play Session Procedures Checklist* (from Session 3)
- CPRT Cliff Notes (from Session 4)

☐ Conduct play session (same time and place):

- Complete *Play Session Notes.*
- Note what you thought you did well, specifically focusing on esteem building responses, and select one skill you want to work on in your next play session.
- If you needed to set a limit, describe what happened and what you said or did.

☐ Additional Assignment:

_____ ***I will bring my video-recording for next week (if video-recording at clinic: my appt. day/time ____).***

CHILD-PARENT-RELATIONSHIP (C-P-R) TRAINING

Esteem-Building Responses: Developing Your Child's Sense of Competence—Session 7

Rule of Thumb: "Never do for a child that which he can do for himself."

When you do, you rob your child of the joy of discovery and the opportunity to feel competent. You will never know what your child is capable of unless you allow him to try!

Parents help their child develop a positive view of "self," not only by providing their child with love and unconditional acceptance, but also by helping their child feel competent and capable. Parents help their child feel competent and capable by first allowing the child to **experience** what it is like to discover, figure out, and problem-solve. Parents show faith in their child and their child's capabilities by allowing him to struggle with a problem, all the while providing encouragement (encouragement vs. praise is covered in detail in Session 8). For most parents, allowing children to struggle is hard—but it is a necessary process for children to truly feel capable. The next step in helping children develop a positive view of self as competent and capable is learning to respond in ways that give children credit for ideas, effort, and accomplishments, without praising.

Esteem-Building Responses to Use in Play Sessions:

"You did it!"	"You decided that was the way that was supposed to fit together."
"You figured it out."	"You know just how you want that to look."
"You like the way that turned out."	"You're not giving up—you're determined to figure that out."
"You decided. . ."	"You've got a plan for how. . ."

Example 1: Child works and works to get the lid off the Play-Doh and finally gets it off.
Parent response: **"You did it!"** (affect in your voice matches child's affect; don't be over-enthusiastic)

Example 2: Child works and works to get the lid off the Play-Doh but can't get it off.
Parent response: **"You're determined to figure that out."**

Example 3: Child struggles to get the dart to fit into the gun and pushed in all the way and finally gets it in.
Parent response: **"You figured it out."**

Example 4: Child spends time drawing, cutting, and gluing a nondescript piece of "art" and shows you with a smile when he is finished.
Parent response: **"You really like the way that turned out."**

Example 5: Child is carefully setting up army soldiers and telling you all about a battle that is going to take place, what is going to happen, and how one side is going to sneak up, and so forth.
Parent response: **"You've got a plan for how that side is going to. . ."** or **"You've got that all planned out."**

Note: *If your child tends to ask you to do things for him without trying first, ask the therapist to role-play how to return responsibility to your child to do things he is capable of figuring out for himself.*

****

The Struggle to Become a Butterfly: A True Story (Author Unknown)

A family in my neighborhood once brought in two cocoons that were just about to hatch. They watched as the first one began to open and the butterfly inside squeezed very slowly and painfully through a tiny hole that it chewed in one end of the cocoon. After lying exhausted for about 10 minutes following its agonizing emergence, the butterfly finally flew out the open window on its beautiful wings.

The family decided to help the second butterfly so that it would not have to go through such an excruciating ordeal. So, as it began to emerge, they carefully sliced open the cocoon with a razor blade, doing the equivalent of a Caesarean section. The second butterfly never did sprout wings, and in about 10 minutes, instead of flying away, it quietly died.

The family asked a biologist friend to explain what had happened. The scientist said that the difficult struggle to emerge from the small hole actually pushes liquids from deep inside the butterfly's body cavity into the tiny capillaries in the wings, where they harden to complete the healthy and beautiful adult butterfly.

Remember: **WITHOUT THE STRUGGLE, THERE ARE NO WINGS!**

CHILD-PARENT-RELATIONSHIP (C-P-R) TRAINING
Positive Character Qualities—Session 7

affectionate	brave	calm	careful
caring	clever	compassionate	confident
considerate	cooperative	courageous	creative
dependable	determined	empathic	energetic
enthusiastic	friendly	fun	generous
gentle	good sport	helpful	honest
humble	insightful	joyful	kind
loving	loyal	modest	neat
patient	persistent	polite	punctual
reliable	resourceful	respectful	responsible
sensitive	sincere	smart	supportive
team player	thoughtful	trustworthy	unique

This chart was adapted from Sandra R. Blackard, M.A.

CHILD-PARENT-RELATIONSHIP (C-P-R) TRAINING
Play Session Notes—Session 7

Play Session # ____________ Date: ____________

Significant Happenings:

What I Learned About My Child:

Feelings Expressed:

Play Themes:

What I Learned About Myself:

My feelings during the play session:

What I think I was best at:

What was hardest or most challenging for me:

Questions or Concerns:

Skill I Want to Focus on in the Next Play Session: ______________________________

CHILD-PARENT-RELATIONSHIP (C-P-R) TRAINING
Play Session Skills Checklist
For In-Class Review of Video-Recorded Play Session—Session 7

Play Session # ________Date: ______________

(*Note: Indicate ✓ in column if skill was used.*)

✓	Skill	Notes/Comments
	Set the Stage/Structured Play Session	
	Conveyed "Be-With" Attitudes Full attention/interested Toes followed nose	
	Allowed Child to Lead Avoided giving suggestions Avoided asking questions Returned responsibility to child	
	Followed Child's Lead Physically on child's level Moved closer when child was involved in play Joined in play when invited	
✓	Reflective Responding Skills:	
	Reflected child's nonverbal play (Tracking)	
	Reflected child's verbalizations (Content)	
	Reflected child's feelings/wants/wishes	
	Voice tone matched child's intensity/affect	
	Responses were brief and interactive	
	Facial expressions matched child's affect	
	Use of Encouragement/Self-Esteem-Building Responses	
	Set Limits, As Needed, Using A-C-T	

Child-Parent Relationship Therapy (CPRT)

Session 8—Treatment Outline

⏱ Time Marker

Note: ***See Companion Website*** *Appendix A to download and print* ***Materials Checklist*** *and any additional materials for this session. Display* ***Dos and Don'ts Poster*** *next to the monitor. The CPRT Training Resources section in this manual provides information about suggested books and videos.*

______ **I. Informal Sharing, followed by Review of Homework and Play Session Reports** (video-recorded parents share last)

- Parents report on the character quality note-writing activity.

  Keep the sharing brief—caution parents not to expect an overt response from their children.

- Parents report on practicing giving a self-esteem-building response outside the play session.

  Parents report on practicing a self-esteem-building response made during play sessions, as a lead into play session reports.

- Parents who did not video this week briefly report on play sessions focusing on parents' perceived changes in their own behavior

  Focus on **Play Session Dos**.

  Use examples from parents' comments to reinforce **Dos**.

  Role-play with parents on how to respond to difficult situations.

  Remember the Donut Analogy: Encourage and Support!

______ **II. Video-Recorded Play Session Review and Supervision**

- View two parent-child play sessions, following same procedure as last week.

  Ask parents to identify the **Dos** they saw demonstrated.

- Refer parents to handout, *Play Session Skills Checklist*, in the *Parent Notebook* p. 164 and ask parents to check off skills they see being demonstrated.

- When you stop video to give feedback, refer to *Play Session Dos & Don'ts* poster/handout.

  Ask parents to identify the **Dos** they saw demonstrated.

______ **III. Review *Encouragement vs. Praise* handout** (*Parent Notebook* p. 162).

- Praise promotes children's dependence on external source of evaluation and motivation in order to be rewarded for behavior, good grades, etc.

- Praise can only be given when a child meets parent's expectation.
- Encouragement promotes self-motivation and internal evaluation by focusing on children's efforts and contributions.
- Encouragement focuses on the child's efforts and hard work and can be given regardless of whether the child meets parent's expectations.
- **Rule of Thumb: "Encourage the effort rather than praise the product."** Children need encouragement like a plant needs water.
- Go over a few examples of encouraging responses in the handout that are most relevant to use in play sessions.

  Note: Of all CPRT skills, parents struggle the most with the concept of using encouragement rather than praise. Reflect their doubts and remind them that you are only asking them to practice using encouragement during play sessions and to begin to find a few times outside of play sessions that they can intentionally use encouraging responses.

_______ IV. Demonstration of Play Session Skills and Encouraging Responses, followed by Role-Play

- Always allow time for parents to see a demonstration of play session skills that you want them to emulate, focusing on those skills they report the most difficulty with.
- After viewing demonstration, ask parents to take turns as a child and parent role-playing scenarios they believe are most difficult for them, including at least one role-play using encouraging responses.

_______ V. Arrange for Two Parents to Video-Record This Week

- Name/phone number _________ day/time (if recording at clinic) _______________
- Name/phone number _________ day/time (if recording at clinic) _______________
- Remind parent(s) who are video-recording this week to make note on their *Parent Notes and Homework* handout.

_______ VI. Homework Assignments (*Parent Notebook* p. 161)

☐ Read *Encouragement vs. Praise*—practice giving at least one encouragement response <u>during</u> your play session. Also, practice giving at least one encouragement <u>outside</u> of your play session.

What happened or what child said (outside of play session) _________________
What you said ____
How child responded (verbally or nonverbally) ____________________________

☐ Write down one issue you are struggling with outside of play session time that you would like help with.

____

☐ Read over handouts prior to play session:

- *Limit Setting: A-C-T Before It's Too Late!* (from Session 4)
- *Play Session Dos & Don'ts* (from Session 3)
- *Play Session Procedures Checklist* (from Session 3)
- CPRT Cliff Notes (from Session 4)

☐ Conduct play session (same time and place):

- Complete *Play Session Notes.*
- Note what you thought you did well, and select one skill you want to work on in your next play session.
- Note use of encouraging responses.

☐ Additional Assignment:

Write second note to your child of focus, as well as other children in the family, pointing out another positive character quality you appreciate about the child. (Vary how the note is delivered, for example, place it in the child's lunchbox, tape it to the mirror in the bathroom, place it on the child's pillow or under the child's dinner plate, etc.)

____ ***I will bring my video next week (if video-recording at clinic: my appt. day/time ____).***

______ **VII. Close with Motivational Poem, Story or Rule of Thumb** (optional)

RULE OF THUMB TO REMEMBER:

"Encourage the effort rather than praise the product!"

Children need encouragement like a plant needs water.

CHILD-PARENT-RELATIONSHIP (C-P-R) TRAINING
Parent Notes and Homework—Session 8

👍 RULE OF THUMB TO REMEMBER:

"Encourage the effort rather than praise the product!"
Children need encouragement like a plant needs water.

Notes: (use back for additional notes)

____

____

____

____

____

____

____

____

Homework Assignments:

- ☐ Read *Encouragement vs. Praise*—practice giving at least one encouragement response during your play session. Also practice giving at least one encouragement outside of your play session.
  What happened or what child said (outside of play session) ______________________
  What you said ______________________________________
  How child responded (verbally or nonverbally) ______________________
- ☐ Write down one issue you are struggling with outside of play session time that you would like help with.
  ____
- ☐ Read over handouts prior to play session:
  - *Limit Setting: A-C-T Before It's Too Late!* (from Session 4)
  - *Play Session Dos & Don'ts* (from Session 3)
  - *Play Session Procedures Checklist* (from Session 3)
  - CPRT Cliff Notes (from Session 4)
- ☐ Conduct play session (same time and place):
  - Complete *Play Session Notes.*
  - Note what you thought you did well, and select one skill you want to work on in your next play session.
  - Note use of encouraging responses used.
- ☐ Additional Assignment:

  Write second note to your child of focus, as well as other children in the family, pointing out another positive character quality you appreciate about the child. (Vary how the note is delivered, for example, place it in the child's lunchbox, tape it to the mirror in the bathroom, place it on the child's pillow or under the child's dinner plate, etc.)

  _____ *I will bring my video next week (if video-recording at clinic: my appt. day/time _____).*

CHILD-PARENT-RELATIONSHIP (C-P-R) TRAINING
Encouragement vs. Praise—Session 8

Rule of Thumb: "Encourage the effort rather than praise the product"

Praise: Although praise and encouragement both focus on positive behaviors and appear to be the same process, praise actually fosters dependence in children by teaching them to rely on an external source of control and motivation rather than on self-control and self-motivation.

- Praise is an attempt to motivate children with external rewards. In effect, the parent who praises is saying, "If you do something I consider good, you will have the reward of being recognized and valued by me."
- Overreliance on praise can produce crippling effects. Children come to believe that their worth depends upon the opinions of others. Praise employs words that place value judgments on children and focuses on external evaluation.

Examples of Praise:

"You're such a good boy/girl." Your child may wonder, "*Am I accepted only when I'm good?*"

"You got an A. That's great!" Your child may wonder, "*Am I worthwhile only when I make As?*"

"You did a good job." "I'm so proud of you." The message sent is that your (parent's) evaluation is more important than your child's.

Encouragement: Focuses on internal evaluation and the contributions children make—facilitates development of self-motivation and self-control. Encouraging parents teach their children to accept their own inadequacies, learn from mistakes (mistakes are wonderful opportunities for learning), have confidence in themselves, and feel useful through contribution.

- When commenting on children's efforts, be careful not to place value judgments on what they have done. Be alert to eliminate value-laden words (good, great, excellent, etc.) from your vocabulary at these times. Instead, substitute words of encouragement that help children believe in themselves.
- Encouragement <u>focuses on effort</u> and <u>can always be given</u>. Children who feel their efforts are encouraged, valued, and appreciated develop qualities of persistence and determination and tend to be good problem-solvers.

Note: Parent's voice should match child's level of affect; if child is excited about getting an "A" on a test, parent responds likewise with excitement in her voice, "You're really proud of that!" Use after-the-event celebrations (based on child's pride in achievement) instead of rewards (external motivators to get the child to achieve) to recognize achievement. In the above example, the parent could add, "Sounds like something to celebrate; let's make a cake!" or "You choose the restaurant, my treat!"

<u>Encouraging Phrases That Recognize Effort and Improvement:</u>

"You did it!" or "You got it!"
"You really worked hard on that."
"You didn't give up until you figured it out."
"Look at the progress you've made. . . " (Be specific.)
"You answer the questions about sports really fast!"

<u>Encouraging Phrases That Show Confidence:</u>

"That's a rough one, but I bet you'll figure it out."
"I have confidence in you. You'll figure it out."
"Sounds like you have a plan."
"Sounds like you know a lot about ____________________________."

<u>Encouraging Phrases That Focus on Contributions, Assets, and Appreciation:</u>

"Thanks, that was a big help."
"It was thoughtful of you to ___________" or "I appreciate that you ___________."
"You have a knack for __________. Can you give me a hand with that?"
"It took a lot of courage to do that and you did it."

<u>In Summary, Encouragement Is:</u>

1. Valuing and accepting children as they are (not putting conditions on acceptance).
2. Pointing out the positive aspects of behavior.
3. Showing faith in children, so that they can come to believe in themselves.
4. Recognizing effort and improvement (rather than requiring achievement).
5. Showing appreciation for contributions.

Adapted from Dinkmeyer, D., & McKay, G.D. (1982). <u>The Parent's Handbook</u>. Circle Pines, MN: American Guidance Service.

CHILD-PARENT-RELATIONSHIP (C-P-R) TRAINING
Play Session Notes—Session 8

Play Session # ________ Date: ________________

Significant Happenings:

What I Learned About My Child:

Feelings Expressed:

Play Themes:

What I Learned About Myself:

My feelings during the play session:

What I think I was best at:

What was hardest or most challenging for me:

Questions or Concerns:

Skill I Want to Focus on in the Next Play Session: ________________________________

CHILD-PARENT-RELATIONSHIP (C-P-R) TRAINING
Play Session Skills Checklist
For In-Class Review of Video-Recorded Play Session—Session 8

Play Session # ________Date: ______________

(Note: Indicate ✓ in column if skill was used.)

✓	Skill	Notes/Comments
	Set the Stage/Structured Play Session	
	Conveyed "Be-With" Attitudes Full attention/interested Toes followed nose	
	Allowed Child to Lead Avoided giving suggestions Avoided asking questions Returned responsibility to child	
	Followed Child's Lead Physically on child's level Moved closer when child was involved in play Joined in play when invited	
	Reflective Responding Skills:	
	Reflected child's nonverbal play (Tracking)	
	Reflected child's verbalizations (Content)	
	Reflected child's feelings/wants/wishes	
	Voice tone matched child's intensity/affect	
	Responses were brief and interactive	
	Facial expressions matched child's affect	
	Use of Encouragement/Self-Esteem-Building Responses	
	Set Limits, As Needed, Using A-C-T	

Child-Parent Relationship Therapy (CPRT)

Session 9—Treatment Outline

⌚ Time Marker

Note: ***See Companion Website*** *Appendix A to download and print* ***Materials Checklist*** *and any additional materials for this session. Display* ***Dos and Don'ts Poster*** *next to the monitor. The CPRT Training Resources section in this manual provides information about suggested books and videos.*

_______ **I. Informal Sharing, followed by Review of Homework and Play Session Reports**

- Parents report on practicing giving an encouragement response during their play session.

  If parents bring up use of encouragement responses outside play sessions, ask them to share those responses when skills outside play sessions are discussed later in the session.

- Parents who did not video this week briefly report on play sessions, focusing on parent's perceived changes in their own behavior.

  Focus on **Play Session Dos** (use poster for parents to refer to).

  Use examples from parents' comments to reinforce **Dos**.

  Role-play with parents on how to respond to difficult situations.

  Remember the Donut Analogy: Encourage and Support!

_______ **II. Video-Recorded Play Session Review and Supervision**

- View two parent-child play sessions, following same procedure as last week. Play video until a strength is evident.
- Model encouragement and facilitate peer feedback.
- Refer parents to handout, *Play Session Skills Checklist*, in the *Parent Notebook* p. 172 and ask parents to check off skills they see being demonstrated.
- Continue to refer to *Play Session Dos & Don'ts* poster/handout.
- As parents bring up questions about limit setting, review limit setting steps and discuss advanced limit-setting strategies to use during play sessions when child does not comply with limit (refer parents to handout, *Advanced Limit Setting: Giving Choices as Consequences for Noncompliance*, in the *Parent Notebook* p. 166).

______ III. Using Skills Outside the Play Session

- Invite parents to comment on homework assignments from Session 8 about using encouragement and other skills outside the play session.
- Review your notes regarding parents' concerns expressed over the past 8 weeks—ask which concerns remain troublesome. Briefly explore use of CPRT skills to address concerns (further discussion in Session 10).
- **Rule of Thumb: "Don't try to change everything at once!"**

  Focus on "big" issues that ultimately will mean the most to your child's development of positive self-esteem and feelings of competence and usefulness.
- Discuss how to use limit setting outside of play sessions (refer parents to handout, *Generalizing Limit Setting to Outside the Play Session*, in the *Parent Notebook* p. 168).

  Review examples with parents.

  Note: This topic typically generates much discussion among parents! Reflect their concerns and assure them that this skill takes practice and patience.
- **Rule of Thumb: "Where there are no limits, there is no security."**

  Consistent Limits = Secure Relationship.

  When you don't follow through, you lose credibility and harm your relationship with your child.
- Parents often report that their child is having difficulty adjusting to new happenings or new routines. Discuss reflecting the child's feelings and concerns, rather than trying to problem solve.

  If time allows, briefly discuss *Structured Doll Play* (Appendix D) and offer to bring the handout for parents next week. Although not a specific CPRT skill, this activity is consistent with the idea of helping children predict what is going to happen and providing them a measure of control.

  Remember: Predictability = Sense of Security and Safety

______ IV. Demonstration of Play Session Skills, followed by Role-Play (if needed)

- Always allow time for parents to see a demonstration of play session skills, if needed. *Note: By this time in CPRT, parents may not need to see a demonstration.*
- Invite parents to role-play a few scenarios they believe are most difficult for them. Limit setting is typically a skill that parents feel less confident about, particularly using the skill outside of play session.

______ V. Arrange for Two Parents to Video-Record This Week

- Name/phone number ________ day/time (if recording at clinic) ______________
- Name/phone number ________ day/time (if recording at clinic) ______________

- Remind parent(s) who are video-recording this week to make note on their *Parent Notes and Homework* handout.

_______ **VI. Homework Assignments** (*Parent Notebook* p. 165)

☐ Review *Advanced Limit Setting* and Generalizing Limit Setting to Outside the Play Session.

Think of a limit setting situation that you anticipate that your child might have difficulty complying with during a play session (or in the past has not complied) and describe on *Advanced Limit Setting* handout and note how you might respond.

☐ Describe a time you used A-C-T outside of the play session this week.

What happened ____
What you said ____
How child responded (verbally or nonverbally) ______________________

☐ Notice the number of times you touch your child in interactions outside the play session (hugging, patting on the head, a touch on the arm, etc.) and keep count this week. # of physical contacts:

☐ A related assignment is to play-wrestle with your children. (Example: In a two-parent family with small children, Mom and kids can sneak up on Dad and try to get him down on the floor, accompanied by lots of fun and laughter.)

☐ Report on use of C-P-R responses used outside of play session this week. What went well and what didn't? ________________________________

☐ Read over handouts prior to play session:

- *Limit Setting: A-C-T Before It's Too Late!* (from Session 4)
- *Play Session Dos & Don'ts* (from Session 3)
- *Play Session Procedures Checklist* (from Session 3)
- CPRT Cliff Notes (from Session 4)

☐ Conduct play session (same time and place):

- Complete *Play Session Notes*.
- Note what you thought you did well, and select one skill you want to work on in your next play session.
- Note any limits setting situations and how you responded.

☐ Additional Assignment:

Write third note to your child of focus, as well as other children in the family, pointing out <u>another</u> positive character quality you appreciate about the child. (Vary how the note is delivered.)

____ ***I will bring my video next week (if video-recording at clinic: my appt. day/time _____).***

_______ **VII. Close with Motivational Poem, Story, or Rule of Thumb** (optional)

☝ RULES OF THUMB TO REMEMBER:

1. **"Where there are no limits, there is no security."** Consistent Limits = Secure Relationship. When you don't follow through, you lose credibility and harm your relationship with your child.
2. **"Don't try to change everything at once!"** Focus on "big" issues that ultimately will mean the most to your child's development of positive self-esteem and feelings of competence.

CHILD-PARENT-RELATIONSHIP (C-P-R) TRAINING
Parent Notes and Homework—Session 9

RULES OF THUMB TO REMEMBER:

1. **"Where there are no limits, there is no security."** Consistent Limits = Security in the Relationship. When you don't follow through, you lose credibility and harm your relationship with your child.
2. **"Don't try to change everything at once!"** Focus on "big" issues that ultimately will mean the most to your child's development of positive self-esteem and feelings of competence.

Notes: (use back for additional notes)

____

____

Homework Assignments:

☐ Review *Advanced Limit Setting* and *Generalizing Limit Setting to Outside the Play Session*. Think of a limit setting situation that you anticipate that your child might have difficulty complying with during a play session (or in the past has not complied) and describe on *Advanced Limit Setting* handout and note how you might respond.

☐ Describe a time you used A-C-T outside of the play session this week.

What happened ____________________

What you said ____________________

How child responded (verbally or nonverbally) ____________________

☐ Notice the number of times you touch your child in interactions outside the play session (hugging, patting on the head, a touch on the arm, etc.) and keep count this week of physical contacts:

____

☐ A related assignment is to play-wrestle with your children. (Example: In a two-parent family with small children, Mom and kids can sneak up on Dad and try to get him down on the floor, accompanied by lots of fun and laughter.)

☐ Report on use of C-P-R responses used outside of play session this week. What went well and what didn't? ____________________

____

☐ Read over handouts prior to play session:

- *Limit Setting: A-C-T Before It's Too Late!* (from Session 4)
- *Play Session Dos & Don'ts* (from Session 3)
- *Play Session Procedures Checklist* (from Session 3)
- *CPRT Cliff Notes* (from Session 4)

☐ Conduct play session (same time and place):

- Complete *Play Session Notes*.
- Note what you thought you did well, and select one skill you want to work on in your next play session.
- Note any limits setting situations and how you responded.

☐ Additional Assignment:
Write third note to your child of focus, as well as other children in the family, pointing out <u>another</u> positive character quality you appreciate about the child. (Vary how the note is delivered.)

____ ***I will bring my video next week (if video-recording at clinic: my appt. day/time _____).***

CHILD-PARENT-RELATIONSHIP (C-P-R) TRAINING

Advanced Limit Setting: Giving Choices as Consequences for Noncompliance—Session 9

Play Session Example: After parent has stated that the Play-Doh is for playing with on the tray, 5-year-old Damian dumps it on the floor.

Step 1. Parent follows the A-C-T method of limit setting: "**Damian, I know that you want to play with the Play-Doh over there, but the floor (carpet, etc.) is not for putting Play-Doh on; (pointing to tray) the tray is for putting the Play-Doh on.**" Damian continues to ignore parent and begins to smash the Play-Doh on the floor.

Step 2. Parent may patiently restate limit up to three times before beginning Step 3.

Note: This example (restating limit up to three times) assumes that parent has chosen a location for the play session where the floor surface can be easily cleaned by parent after special playtime.

Step 3. "If-Then" choices (consequences) for following or not following limit.

Begin "If-Then" choice-giving method to provide consequence for unacceptable behavior. Note the number of times the words "choose" or "choice" are used! Remember that the intent is for the child to bring himself under control; therefore, patience is the order of the day. Children need time and practice to learn self-control.

Example: "**Damian, If you choose to play with the Play-Doh on the tray (pointing to tray), then you choose to play with the Play-Doh today. If you choose to continue to play with the Play-Doh on the floor, then you choose not to play with the Play-Doh for the rest of today.**" (Pause.)

- Patiently restate if child does not make the choice to comply with the limit. (If Damian doesn't answer and continues to play with Play-Doh on floor, then he has made his choice.) "**Damian, it looks like you've chosen to put the Play-Doh up for today. You can choose to give me the Play-Doh, or you can choose for me to put the Play-Doh up for you; which do you choose?**"
- If child begins to cry and beg for the Play-Doh, parent must be tough and follow through, acknowledging child's feelings and giving child hope that he will have a chance to make a different choice in the next play session. "**Damian, I understand that you're unhappy that you chose to have the Play-Doh put up for today, but you can choose to play with it in our next play time.**"

In the above example, if at any point the child took the Play-Doh and put it on the tray to play with, the parent must be careful to respond matter-of-factly, "**Looks like you decided you wanted to play with it some more time.**"

Practice:

1. Your child aims a loaded dart gun at you.

   A *[Child's name], I know you'd like to shoot me*__________________.

   C *but I'm not for shooting*____________________________.

   T *You can shoot the bop bag or the doll (pointing at each)*__________.

Your child continues to aim the gun at you after you have set the limit using A-C-T three times.

[Child's name], if you choose to *aim the gun at me,*
then you choose *not to play with the gun today.*

If your child continues to aim the gun at you (whether he shoots the gun or not), you say: [Child's name], *looks like you've chosen not to play with the gun for the rest of today.*

If your child shoots the gun at the bop bag or another acceptable place, you say (matter-of-factly): *Looks like you have chosen to play with the gun some more today.*

2. Describe a situation in which you think you might need to set a limit during the play session and you anticipate the child might not comply.

Situation: ____

____

____

____

A ____

C ____

T ____

If/Then ____

____

____

____

____

____

CHILD-PARENT-RELATIONSHIP (C-P-R) TRAINING
Generalizing Limit Setting to Outside the Play Session—Session 9

Acknowledge the feeling

Communicate the limit

Target alternatives

Example # 1

Your 6-year-old child, Olivia, wants a My Little Pony stuffed toy from the "claw" game at the movie theater. The rest of your family is walking into the theater and Olivia is standing cross-armed, insisting on playing the game.

1. Acknowledge your child's feelings (*your voice must convey genuine empathy and understanding*).

   "Olivia, I know you *really* want to play that." (She learns her feelings and desires are valid and acceptable.)
2. Communicate the limit (be specific, clear, and brief).

   "But, it's not game time; *It's movie time!*" (this response may be enough to help Olivia bring self under control and go into the movie with you)
3. Target acceptable alternatives. (Provide one or more choices, depending on age of child.)

   "You can choose to walk with me into the movie or you can choose to walk with Daddy and Joey into the movie." (If you are <u>not</u> okay with her playing the game at all.)

   Or

   "You can choose to play that after the movie." (If you are okay with her playing the game.)

Note: The goal of targeting alternatives is to provide your child with acceptable alternatives—ones that are acceptable to your child and you (parent), and ones that you believe will help child get their needs met. In the above example, Olivia wanted to do something fun and also maybe wanted to decide how things went that day. With the alternatives presented, Olivia's need for fun and decision making power were both met (movie and choice).

TIP: Simply recognizing and acknowledging your child's feelings and desires can often defuse the intensity of the feeling or need.

- Oftentimes, children have emotional needs underneath the surface of the situation. Olivia may have been feeling left out that day. So, her insistence about playing the game may be less about the prize and more about wanting to be attended to relationally. Acknowledging her feelings and presenting alternatives to *Be-With* others would help meet this underlying need for relationship.
- Patiently restate the limit up to three times, depending on the age of the child, to allow child to struggle with self-control before proceeding to the next step.

4. Choice giving (consequences) as next step after noncompliance. Example: Olivia continues to refuse to walk into the movie and insists on playing the game now.

"Olivia, playing this game now is not one of the choices. <u>You can choose</u> to see the movie and <u>choose</u> to play the game afterwards, or <u>you can choose</u> to stay here with me and be late for the movie, and <u>choose</u> not to play the game afterwards."

If child starts walking away, even slowly, parent may state: **"That was a hard decision for you. Looks like you are choosing to watch the movie now and play the game later."**

If child does not choose, parent may state: **"If you choose to not choose, you choose for me to choose for you."**

If child continues to insist on playing the game now, parent can state: **"I see you've chosen to stay out here with me and to not play the game later."**

TIP: When child pushes limits, parent increases empathy and understanding of how hard it is to choose! Before the situation escalates into choices as consequences, be sure to give child ample time to relax and make a choice.

Remember the **Rule of Thumb: "When a child is drowning, don't try to teach her to swim."** In this moment of stress, Olivia is in fight-flight-or-freeze mode, neurobiologically, and therefore needs you to **Connect** and acknowledge her feelings and be patient in order for her to relax enough to be able to engage her prefrontal cortex to make a choice. After all, your goal is not to "win"—the goal of limit setting is for you (parent) to provide your child with consistent opportunity to develop internal coping strategies and decision-making skills.

- In this example, even the last choice of spending time with her parent (if parent is okay with being late to the movie) and not playing the game presents Olivia with the opportunity for quality time with her parent. If after Olivia relaxes in the lobby, she says, "*Mommy, can we go watch the movie now and play the game after?*" You respond empathically: ***"Remember when you chose to stay here with me instead of going into the movie—at that very moment, you chose to not play the game today, but we can go watch the movie now."*** Your child may continue to plead and cry (because it has worked in the past). BE FIRM—don't give in! Your child's *choices* matter.

What To Do After A-C-T

After you've followed the three-step A-C-T process with empathy and firmness:

1. If you are satisfied with your response to the child's question and the question or plea is repeated, DON'T DISCUSS FURTHER.
2. If you think the child doesn't understand your response, say:

   — "I've already answered that question. You must have some question about my answer."
3. If you think the child understands, say:

   — "I can tell you'd like to discuss this some more, but I've already answered that question."

   OR

   — "I can tell you don't like my answer. If you are asking again because you want me to change my mind, I will not."

   OR

   — "Do you remember the answer I gave you a few minutes ago when you asked that same question?" If child answers, "No, I don't remember," say, "Go sit down in a quiet place and think. I know you'll be able to remember."

4. If you are not satisfied with your response to your child's question:

   — If you are open to persuasion, say:

   "I don't know. Let's sit down and discuss it."

   — If you intend to answer the question later but are not prepared to answer now, say:

   "I can't answer that question now because (I want to talk it over with someone; I want to get more information; I want to think about it, etc.). I'll let you know (specific time)."

   — If child demands an answer now, say:

   "If you must have an answer now, the answer will have to be 'NO."

What To Do When Limit Setting Doesn't Work

You have been careful several times to calmly and empathically use **A-C-T and Choice-Giving**. Your child continues to deliberately disobey. What do you do?

- ☐ Look for natural causes for rebellion: Fatigue, sickness, hunger, stress, and so forth. Take care of physical needs and crises before expecting cooperation.
- ☐ Remain in control, respecting yourself and your child: You are not a failure if your child rebels, and your child is not bad. All kids need to "practice" rebelling. Remember: At this very moment, nothing is more important than your relationship with your child, so respond in a way that respects your child and yourself. *If you find yourself feeling angry at your child and losing control, walk outside or to another room.*
- ☐ Remember the Brain: Sometimes children can become so dysregulated that they are not capable in the moment of making a choice. The hand model of the brain by Dr. Dan Siegel is an excellent reminder of how to understand and support young children during these times. Can access at this link: https://www.youtube.com/watch?v=gm9CIJ74Oxw
- ☐ Set reasonable consequences for disobedience: Let your child choose to obey or disobey, but set a reason¬able consequence for disobedience. Example: "If you choose to watch TV instead of going to bed, then you choose to give up TV all day tomorrow" (or whatever is a meaningful consequence for child).
- ☐ Never tolerate violence: Physically restrain your child who becomes violent, without becoming aggressive your¬self. Empathically and calmly **REFLECT** your child's anger and loneliness; provide compassionate control and alternatives as child begins to regain control.
- ☐ If your child refuses to choose, you choose for them: Your child's refusal to choose is also a choice. Set the con¬sequences. Example: "If you choose not to (choice A or B), then you have chosen for me to choose for you."
- ☐ ENFORCE THE CONSEQUENCES: Don't state consequences that you cannot enforce. If you crumble under your child's anger or tears, you have abdicated your role as parent and lost your power. **GET TOUGH!** When you don't follow through, you lose credibility and harm your relationship with your child.
- ☐ Recognize signs of more serious problems: Depression, trauma (abuse/neglect/extreme grief/stress). The chronically angry or rebellious child is in emotional trouble and may need professional help. Share your con¬cern with your child. Example: "John, I've noticed that you seem to be angry and unhappy most of the time. I love you, and I'm worried about you. We're going to get help so we can all be happier."

CHILD-PARENT-RELATIONSHIP (C-P-R) TRAINING
Play Session Notes—Session 9

Play Session # ________ Date: ________________

Significant Happenings:

What I Learned About My Child:

Feelings Expressed:

Play Themes:

What I Learned About Myself:

My feelings during the play session:

What I think I was best at:

What was hardest or most challenging for me:

Questions or Concerns:

Skill I Want to Focus on in the Next Play Session: ________________________________

CHILD-PARENT-RELATIONSHIP (C-P-R) TRAINING
Play Session Skills Checklist
For In-Class Review of Video-Recorded Play Session—Session 9

Play Session # ________Date: ______________

(Note: Indicate ✓ in column if skill was used.)

✓	Skill	Notes/Comments
	Set the Stage/Structured Play Session	
	Conveyed "Be-With" Attitudes Full attention/interested Toes followed nose	
	Allowed Child to Lead Avoided giving suggestions Avoided asking questions Returned responsibility to child	
	Followed Child's Lead Physically on child's level Moved closer when child was involved in play Joined in play when invited	
	Reflective Responding Skills:	
	Reflected child's nonverbal play (Tracking)	
	Reflected child's verbalizations (Content)	
	Reflected child's feelings/wants/wishes	
	Voice tone matched child's intensity/affect	
	Responses were brief and interactive	
	Facial expressions matched child's affect	
	Use of Encouragement/Self-Esteem-Building Responses	
	Set Limits, As Needed, Using A-C-T	

Child-Parent Relationship Therapy (CPRT)

Session 10—Treatment Outline

⏱ Time Marker

Note: See ***Companion Website*** *Appendix A to download and print* ***Materials Checklist*** *and any additional materials for this session. Also print* ***Dos and Don'ts Poster****, Appendix C, and display next to the monitor. The CPRT Training Resources section in this manual provides information about suggested books and videos.*

_______ **I. Informal Sharing, followed by Review of Homework and Play Session Reports**

- Parents report on number of times they physically touched their child.
- Invite parents to discuss play-wrestling experience.

_______ **II. Show Last Video(s) and Briefly Debrief Play Sessions**

- Comment on observed growth and change in both parent and child.
- What part of training was most helpful?
- What was hardest for you?
- Any other concerns or issues?

_______ **III. Review Handout: *Rules of Thumb and Other Things to Remember***
(*Parent Notebook* p. 175)

- Ask parents to share the Rule of Thumb that has been most meaningful for them.

_______ **IV. Closing Process**

- Parents share most significant learnings.
- Parents discuss how they perceive their children now as compared with 10 weeks ago.
- Review your notes from *Parent Information Form*.

  Encourage feedback from parents on positive changes in themselves and their children.

  Ask parents to consider if their children have really changed that much or have the parents' perception changed, i.e., become more accepting?

_______ **V. Decide on a Date and Time for Follow-Up Meetings**

Ask for a volunteer to coordinate and suggest parents write the date, time, and volunteer name in blanks provided on their homework sheet:

- Date and time for follow-up meetings: ____________________

- Volunteer meeting coordinator: ______________________________

- Make sure parents (with consent) give phone numbers to the coordinator to make a phone list.

- Optional: Date and time for follow-up with therapist: ______________

______ **VI. Homework Assignments: Emphasize the Importance of Continuing Play Sessions** (*Parent Notebook* p. 173)

☐ Make arrangements as needed for parents who want to continue play sessions with the child of focus and/or begin special playtime with a child other than their child of focus.

☐ Hand out additional appointment cards as needed.

☐ Schedule additional professional help for parents and/or children needing such help.

☐ Continue play sessions: If you stop now, the message is that you were playing with your child because you had to, not because you wanted to.

I agree to continue my play sessions with my child of focus for ________ weeks and/or begin sessions with _______________ and do for ______________________ weeks.

Rule of Thumb: "Good things come in small packages."

Don't wait for big events to enter into your child's world—the little ways are always with us. Hold onto precious moments!

______ **VII. Recommended Reading:**

For Parents

- *Relational Parenting* (2000) and *How to Really Love Your Child* (1992), Ross Campbell

- *Between Parent and Child* (1956), Haim Ginott

- *Liberated Parents, Liberated Children* (1990), Adele Faber and Elaine Mazlish

- *How to Talk So Kids Will Listen and Listen So Kids Will Talk* (2012), Adele Faber and Elaine Mazlish

- *"SAY WHAT YOU SEE" for Parents and Teachers* (2005), Sandra Blackard (Free online resource available at www.languageoflistening.com)

- *The Parent Survival Guide* (2009), Theresa Kellam

- *The Whole-Brain Child: 12 Revolutionary Strategies to Nurture Your Child's Developing Mind* (2011), Daniel Siegel and Tina Payne Bryson

- *No Drama Discipline: The Whole-Brain Way to Calm the Chaos and Nurture Your Child's Developing Mind* (2014), Daniel Siegel and Tina Payne Bryson

- *Parenting from the Inside Out* (2014), Daniel Siegel and Mary Hartzell
- *Brain Based Parenting* (2012), Daniel Hughes and Jonathan Baylin
- *Positive Discipline* (2006), Jane Nelson

For Children

- *No Matter What*, Debi Gliori
- *Love You Forever*, Robert Munsch
- *A Mother's Wish*, Kathy-Jo Wargin
- *The Dot*, Peter Reynolds
- *What Do You Do With an Idea?* Kobi Yamada
- *Not a Box*, Antoinette Portis
- *I Wish You More*, Amy Krouse Rosenthal
- *The Kissing Hand*, Audrey Penn
- *Guess How Much I Love You*, Sam McBratney
- *The Invisible String*, Patrice Karst
- *My Many Colored Days*, Dr. Seuss
- *Alexander and the Terrible, Horrible, No Good, Very Bad Day*, Judith Viorst

_____ **VIII. Hand Out *Certificate of Completion* to Each Parent**

_____ **IX. Close with Motivational Poem, Story, or Rule of Thumb** (optional)

RULE OF THUMB:

"Good things come in small packages."

Don't wait for big events to enter into your child's world—the little ways are always with us. Hold onto precious moments!

CHILD-PARENT-RELATIONSHIP (C-P-R) TRAINING
Parent Notes and Homework—Session 10

RULES OF THUMB TO REMEMBER:

"Good things come in small packages."
Don't wait for big events to enter into your child's world
the little ways are always with us. Hold onto precious moments!
Always remember: "Nothing at this moment is more important than my relationship with my child."
(Also applies to significant others)

Notes: (use back for additional notes)

____

____

____

____

____

____

Homework Assignments:

- ☐ Continue play sessions: If you stop now, the message is that you were playing with your child because you had to, not because you wanted to:
- ☐ **I agree to continue my play sessions with my child of focus for ___ weeks and/or begin sessions with ______________________ and do for ___ weeks.**
- ☐ Date and time for follow-up meetings: ______________________
- ☐ Volunteer meeting coordinator: ______________________

Recommended Reading:

For Parents

- *Relational Parenting* (2000) and *How to Really Love Your Child* (1992), Ross Campbell
- *Between Parent and Child* (1956), Haim Ginott
- *Liberated Parents, Liberated Children* (1990), Adele Faber and Elaine Mazlish
- *How to Talk So Kids Will Listen and Listen So Kids Will Talk* (2012), Adele Faber and Elaine Mazlish
- *"SAY WHAT YOU SEE" for Parents and Teachers* (2005), Sandra Blackard (free online resource available at www.languageoflistening.com)
- *The Parent Survival Guide* (2009), Theresa Kellam
- *The Whole-Brain Child: 12 Revolutionary Strategies to Nurture Your Child's Developing Mind* (2011), Daniel Siegel and Tina Payne Bryson

- *No Drama Discipline: The Whole-Brain Way to Calm the Chaos and Nurture Your Child's Developing Mind* (2014), Daniel Siegel and Tina Payne Bryson
- *Parenting from the Inside Out* (2014), Daniel Siegel and Mary Hartzell
- *Brain Based Parenting* (2012), Daniel Hughes and Jonathan Baylin
- *Positive Discipline* (2006), Jane Nelson

For Children

- *No Matter What*, Debi Gliori
- *Love You Forever*, Robert Munsch
- *A Mother's Wish*, Kathy-Jo Wargin
- *The Dot*, Peter Reynolds
- *What Do You Do with an Idea?* Kobi Yamada
- *Not a Box*, Antoinette Portis
- *I Wish You More*, Amy Krouse Rosenthal
- *The Kissing Hand*, Audrey Penn
- *Guess How Much I Love You*, Sam McBratney
- *The Invisible String*, Patrice Karst
- *My Many-Colored Days*, Dr. Seuss
- *Alexander and the Terrible, Horrible, No Good, Very Bad Day*, Judith Viorst

CHILD-PARENT-RELATIONSHIP (C-P-R) TRAINING
Rules of Thumb and Other Things to Remember—Session 10

Rules of Thumb

1. **Focus on the donut, not the hole!**
Focus on the relationship (your strengths and your child's strengths), NOT the problem.
2. **Be a thermostat, not a thermometer!**
Learn to RESPOND (reflect) rather than REACT. Your child's feelings are not your feelings. Your feelings and behavior need not escalate with your child's.
3. **What's most important may not be what you do, but what you do after what you have done!**
We are certain to make mistakes, but we can recover. It is how we handle our mistakes that makes the difference.
4. **Your toes should follow your nose.**
Body language conveys interest.
5. **You can't give away what you do not possess.**
(*Analogy: oxygen mask on airplane*) You can't extend patience and acceptance to your child if you can't first offer it to yourself.
6. **When a child is drowning, don't try to teach her to swim.**
When a child is feeling upset or out of control, that is not the moment to impart a rule or teach a lesson.
7. **During play sessions, limits are not needed until they are needed!**
8. **If you can't say it in 10 words or less, don't say it.**
As parents, we tend to over-explain, and our message gets lost in the words.
9. **Grant in fantasy what you can't grant in reality.**
In a play session, it is okay to act out feelings and wishes that in reality may require limits.
10. **Big choices for big kids, little choices for little kids.**
Choices given must be commensurate with child's developmental stage.
11. **Never do for a child that which he can do for himself.**
You will never know what your child is capable of unless you allow him to try!
12. **Encourage the effort rather than praise the product.**
Children need encouragement like a plant needs water.
13. **Don't try to change everything at once!**
Focus on "big" issues that ultimately will mean the most to your child's development of positive self-esteem and feelings of competence.
14. **Where there are no limits, there is no security.** (Consistent Limits = Secure Relationship)
When you don't follow through, you lose credibility and harm your relationship with your child.
15. **Good things come in small packages.**
Don't wait for big events to enter into your child's world—the little ways are always with us. Hold on to precious moments!

CHILD-PARENT-RELATIONSHIP (C-P-R) TRAINING
Page 2—Rules of Thumb and Other Things to Remember—Session 10

Other Things to Remember:

1. Reflective responses help children to feel understood and can lessen anger.
2. In play, children express what their lives are like now, what their needs are, or how they wish things could be. Children with a history of traumatic experiences may play out past events as they experience them in the present.
3. In the playtimes, the parent is not the source of answers (reflect questions back to the child: "Hmm—I wonder").
4. Don't ask questions you already know the answer to.
5. Questions imply non-understanding. Questions put children in their minds. Children live in their hearts.
6. What's important is not what the child knows, but what the child believes.
7. When you focus on the problem, you lose sight of the child.
8. Support the child's feeling, intent, or need, even if you can't support the child's behavior.
9. Noticing the child is a powerful builder of self-esteem.
10. Empower children by giving them credit for making decisions: "You decided to ________."
11. One of the best things we can communicate to our children is that they are competent. Tell children they are capable, and they will think they are capable. If you tell children enough times they can't do something, sure enough, they can't.
12. Encourage creativity and freedom—with freedom comes responsibility.
13. "We're about to institute a new and significant policy immediately effective within the confines of this domicile."
14. When we are flexible in our approach, we can handle anger much more easily. When parents are rigid in their approach, both parent and child can end up hurt.
15. When unsure of what to say to your child or what to do, ask yourself, "What action or words will most preserve the relationship or do least harm?" Sometimes walking away and saying nothing, or telling the child, "I need to take a time-out to cool off, and then we can talk," is best. Always remember: "Nothing at this moment is more important than my relationship with my child." (Also applies to spouses, significant others, etc.)
16. Live in the moment—today is enough. Don't push children toward the future.

CPRT TODDLER MODEL

Mary Morrison Bennett and Kara Carnes-Holt

CPRT TODDLER MODEL

Mary Morrison Bennett and Kara Carnes-Holt

This chapter provides an overview of the CPRT-Toddler protocol for parents of children ages 1½ to 3 years. **The complete CPRT-Toddler Therapist Protocol and Parent Notebook are found on the accompanying Companion Website at www.routledge.com/cw/bratton.** The protocol is designed for use by mental health professionals trained and certified in the CPRT model.

Adapting CPRT for toddlers can assist parents in developmentally appropriate expectations and the creation of secure attuned relationships with their young child. Understanding children and their developmental stages and tasks is essential when creating interventions that are appropriate to the level of development and comprehension of the child (Weiner & Robinson-Kurpuis, 1995). According to Siegel and Hartzell (2004), relationships that provide experiences of connection, safety, and understanding promote secure attachments. Therefore, it is essential that parents of toddlers learn the therapeutic skills necessary to meet their child's need to form a secure attachment. CPRT-Toddler directly addresses the training and development of these therapeutic skills.

The CPRT-Toddler therapist should be prepared to provide empathy and understanding to the weary caregivers with whom they work. Therapists will need to be especially empathetic with caregivers' perspectives. As parents in the group share their experiences, the therapist will sensitively reflect feeling and connect group members to facilitate support among members.

Physical, Emotional, and Cognitive Development

The first 3 years of life are full of significant development in all areas for young children. Rogers (1951) proposed that all children are born with the innate desire to grow and learn to connect with people and their environment. Perry and Szalavitz (2006) concluded that the experiences children encounter can enhance or deter their development and that parents and other primary caregivers play an important role in influencing a child's development. The most important thing parents can offer children are contained in the natural, unhurried, and sensitive responses that come from "being with" their child (Thompson, 2001).

Child development has been extensively studied, and it has been determined there is a typical pattern of development, that given time, most children will progress through the stages of development, often at predictable times (NAEYC, 2009). Although the stages of development are sequential, children move through them at their own pace. Caregivers may be concerned about their child who is not moving through the developmental stages as quickly as they would like or not doing the same tasks as their nephew at that age. Caregivers may ask, "Is my child normal?" It is the therapist's responsibility to be attentive to these parents and help them understand the importance of developmental tasks and respecting their child's pace (Ray, 2016).

One general piece of development knowledge we have found helpful for parents is the concept of disintegration. As children develop, they may unexpectedly seem to regress in a particular skill, just before the integration of new skills. Caregivers may report the child is falling apart and suddenly cannot do things they previously could. Then once integration is complete, the child has several new skills (Davies, 2011). This is because the human brain can only concentrate on one thing at a time. If a child is growing in one area, all the brain's energy is going toward that growth and cannot attend to other areas of development (Wood, 2015). Gesell (Gesell Institute of Child Development, 2011) referred to stages as either being periods of equilibrium or disequilibrium. Periods of equilibrium are described as calm, confident, and compliant while periods of disequilibrium are described as explosive, fearful, and self-focused. Caregivers also benefit from knowing to expect horizontal growth versus vertical growth. Some parents create a hierarchical view of development and value some skills more than others, such as verbal skills commonly associated with an increased intelligence, which is simply not the case. Assisting caregivers in understanding that children develop in different areas at different rates helps them to understand their child more.

The CPRT-Toddler therapist will explain to parents pertinent developmental issues as they apply the parents' concerns. Toddlers are entering a phase where they desire more independence; they want to "help" parents complete tasks. Toddlers desire to experience the moment and adults desire to complete the task. During this phase, the toddler gains some self-control and desires to be separate from the caregiver.

According to Loevinger's (1997) theory of ego development, children aged 2–5 years are in the "impulsive" stage of ego development, their emotional range is small, and their focus is on immediate needs as well as needs only impacting them directly. This immediacy can be a challenge when parents need their child to get dressed and leave for school, but the child is concerned about arranging cars on the shelf and school is not his immediate need. When the CPRT therapist explains this is typical development for children this age, parents are able to set their expectations more appropriately, which ultimately positively impacts their relationship with their child.

Parents of children who are more physical, coordinated, and often taller may wonder why their child does not have an expansive vocabulary. As a CPRT-Toddler therapist, it is critical to have an understanding of emotional, cognitive, and physical development of young children in order to alleviate parents' anxiety and help them set up appropriate expectations of their child. Managing expectations is a critical component of parenthood.

Brain Development

Brain development during the toddler stage has a primary focus of integration of numerous functions such as perceptual, cognitive, and language, and child-led play is an important component in this process (Davies, 2011). The brain develops over time with constant repetition and exposure, and each experience can reinforce positive or negative behaviors (Perry & Szalavitz, 2006). During the toddler stage, a high degree of brain plasticity is present that supports learning and flexibility and the ability to reorganize and respond to a variety of experiences and environmental conditions. Early experiences for young children are highly influential regarding how the brain structures. For example, emotional development is strengthened when caregivers use emotional language such as mad, happy, and sad when interacting with a young child (Woolfolk & Perry, 2015). Simple reflections to toddlers such as "You feel excited grandma is coming!" or "You are angry that your favorite toy broke" assists with optimal brain development as opposed to trying to solve the problem or excessive questioning.

Secure attachment develops in the midst of an attuned relationship that facilitates repeated experiences of love, safety, and trust. The rapid development of the amygdala primarily takes place in children ages 0–36 months (Perry & Szalavitz, 2006). The amygdala is a part of the basal ganglia and is involved with emotional regulation, often referred to as controlling the fight/flight and freeze responses. It can be helpful to parents to recognize this behavior is most likely a freeze response rooted in fear and not simply defiance. Often when parents receive this knowledge about the brain, it helps the parent to be more emotionally responsive to the child. The skills taught in CPRT, such as reflection of feeling, can assist in the crucial development of self-regulation. Therapeutic and relational responsiveness, the focus of CPRT, assists in the parent/toddler attachment dance that promotes the development of a healthy stress response system.

Attachment Development

Infants born into this world are dependent on their primary caregiver for survival. The core of the attachment relationship is a matching and attuned relationship. Attachment is the "reciprocal, enduring, emotional, and physical affiliation between child and a caregiver. The child receives what she needs to live and grow through this relationship, and the caregiver meets her needs to provide sustenance and guidance" (James, 1994, p. 2). CPRT-Toddler focuses on promoting a relationship that is consistent with the "Be-With attitudes" and is emotionally responsive. For example, the skills of reflecting feelings in statement form communicates to toddlers on an emotional level and allows toddlers to feel heard and understood. A secure foundation of a safe, predictable, and dependent relationship provides the needed socio-emotional framework for individuation and independence (Schore, 1994). This attachment relationship develops the framework for the child's perception of the world, relationships, and self-concept.

Healthy attachment enhances the child's ability to feel safe and secure and to self-regulate. The primary caregiver's ability to meet the basic needs of an infant in a genuinely nurturing and consistent manner is basic to the formation of a secure attachment. It is unrealistic to expect parents to be in complete attunement all of the time (Tronick, 2007). CPRT-Toddler focuses on teaching caregivers how to be sensitive to windows of time, such as a special playtime, to practice skills with toddlers such as esteem building, feeling refection, and basic noticing of the child's actions. These skills assist with the ongoing development of a securely attached relationship and assists parents with becoming more emotionally attuned to their child. Secure attachments are thought to develop from an attuned and predictable relationship, such as the CPRT-Toddler special playtimes in which the child has repeated experiences of feeling understood, connected, and protected by the parent. This secure attachment provides the resources for the child to develop meaningful interpersonal relationships in the future (Siegel & Hartzell, 2003).

Modifications for CPRT-Toddlers

It is important that CPRT therapists are thoroughly familiar with the CPRT-Toddler Model chapter in the second edition of the CPRT text (Landreth & Bratton, 2019). **The CPRT-Toddler protocol found on the accompanying Companion Website** details specific adaptations to session outlines, handouts, and toys as well as developmentally sensitive responses appropriate for use with very young children. There are some general adjustments that need to be made to the special playtime. Due to the short attention span of children ages 18 months to 3 years, the length and fluidity of location of special playtime for toddlers is a significant deviation from the standard CPRT model. The younger the child, the shorter the special playtime should be. For children closer to 18 months, having special playtimes three times a week for approximately 10 minutes each time is recommended. For children 2 years old, 15 minutes twice a week is needed, and the closer the child is to 3 years old, 20 minutes once a week.

The toy kit is a significant modification for this developmental stage. For children 1–2 years of age, parents may consider using bath time or water playtime as their special playtime. Children love to splash and parents can reflect, "You made that splash," "Splashing is fun," "You know how to pour water into the cup." Parents should use their discretion in choosing toys. Some children put toys in their mouth at this age, and others do not. Therefore, toys with small parts should be avoided.

Conclusion

The CPRT-Toddler Model is designed to enhance the parent-child relationship. In learning these skills, parents can have a greater understanding of their children and learn to see the world through their child's eyes, therefore increasing empathy and understanding of how their child experiences the world. CPRT therapists have a unique opportunity to support parents in developing their relationship during this critical time of development.

References

Davies, D. (2011). *Child development: A practitioner's guide* (3rd ed.). New York, NY: Guilford.

Gesell Institute of Child Development. (2011). *Gesell developmental observation-revised examiner's manual*. New Haven, CT: Gesell Institute.

James, B. (1994). *Handbook for treatment of attachment-trauma problems in children*. Lexington, MA: Lexington Books.

Landreth, G. L., & Bratton, S. C. (2020). *Child-parent relationship therapy treatment manual* (2nd ed.). New York, NY: Routledge.

Loevinger, J. (1997). Stages of personality development. In R. Hogan, J. Johnson, & S. Briggs (Eds.), *Handbook of personality psychology* (pp. 199–208). San Diego, CA: Academic Press.

National Association for the Education of Young Children. (2009). *NAEYC developmentally appropriate practice in early childhood programs serving children from birth through age 8*. Washington, DC. Retrieved from www.naeyc.org/files/naeyc/file/positions/PSDAP.pdf

Perry, B. D., & Szalavitz, M. (2006). *The boy who was raised as a dog and other stories from a child psychiatrist's notebook*. New York, NY: Basic Books.

Ray, D. C. (2016). An overview of child development. In D. Ray (Ed.), *A therapist's guide to child development: The extraordinarily normal years* (pp. 3–13). New York, NY: Routledge.

Rogers, C. (1951). *Client-centered therapy*. Boston: Houghton Mifflin.

Schore, A. N. (1994). *Affect regulation and the origin of self*. Mahwah, NJ: Erlbaum.

Siegel, D., & Hartzell, M. (2003). *Parenting from the inside out: How a deeper self-understanding can help you raise children who thrive*. New York, NY: Penguin Group.

Siegel, D., & Hartzell, M. (2004). *Parenting from the inside-out: How a deeper self-understanding can help you raise children who thrive*. New York, NY: Jeremy P. Tarcher/Putnam.

Thompson, R. A. (2001). Development in the first years of life. *The Future of Children, 11*(1), 20–33. Retrieved from http://search.proquest.com/docview/220152495?accountid=5683

Tronick, E. (2007). *The neurobehavioral and social-emotional development of infants and children*. New York, NY: Norton.

Weiner, N., & Robinson-Kurpuis, S. E. (1995). *Shattered innocence: A practical guide for counseling women survivors of childhood sexual abuse*. Washington, DC: Taylor & Francis.

Wood, C. (2015). *Yardsticks: Children in the classroom ages 4–14* (3rd ed.). Turners Falls, MA: Center for Responsive Schools.

Woolfolk, A., & Perry, N. (2015). *Child and adolescent development* (2nd ed). Upper Saddle River, NJ: Pearson.

CPRT PREADOLESCENT MODEL

Peggy L. Ceballos, Kara Carnes-Holt, and Kristin K. Meany-Walen

CPRT PREADOLESCENT MODEL

Peggy L. Ceballos, Kara Carnes-Holt, and Kristin K. Meany-Walen

This chapter provides an overview of the CPRT-Preadolescent protocol for parents of children ages 9 to 13 years. **The complete CPRT-Preadolescent Therapist Protocol and Parent Notebook are found on the accompanying Companion Website at www.routledge.com/cw/bratton.** The protocol is designed for use by mental health professionals trained and certified in the CPRT model.

The emerging literature supports that a strong parent-child relationship during preadolescence serves as a protective factor against behavioral problems (Lederman & Mian, 2003) and facilitates optimal development for preadolescents (Papalia, Olds, & Feldman, 2007). However, parents report feeling unprepared to deal with the changes that their preadolescents go through (Baril, Cromer, & McHale, 2007), and preadolescents report feeling misunderstood by their parents (Bulanda & Majumdar, 2008). In response, CPRT can serve to strengthen the parent-child relationship during this important developmental stage. Although the underlying philosophical principles of CPRT apply equally to relationships between preadolescents and their parents as they do to parents of young children, the CPRT-Preadolescent protocol includes several modifications to ensure the training is developmentally responsive.

Developmental Characteristics of Preadolescents

Preadolescence is a developmental phase in which youth are transitioning from childhood into adolescence and might be referred to as early adolescents, preteens, or tweens. A specific age range is not agreed upon by developmental experts but generally consists of ages 9–13 (Meany-Walen, Carnes Holt, Ceballos, & Michero, 2014). Recently, developmental experts have acknowledged and outlined some of the unique characteristics of this age group and how to respond to those changes in ways that fosters growth and maturity (e.g., Center for Disease Control [CDC], 2016).

Social/Emotional

A basic human need is belonging and acceptance (Maslow, 1962). For young children, parents fill this need; however, as children mature, peers begin to serve this role (CDC, 2016). Preadolescents begin to spend more time with friends outside of the home and they become increasingly reliant on peers for support (Kretschmer, Sentse, Kornelis Dijkstra, & Veenstra, 2014). Although preadolescents start to take interest in extra-curricular activities, they may start to dislike school and feel increased stress as academic challenges increase (CDC, 2016). The balancing act of polarizing expectations and experiences might increase their shift in moods and self-esteem (CDC, 2016).

Physical

Preadolescents' bodies begin to grow upward and outward as they become taller and stronger. They may start puberty, experience voice changes, and have an increase in body odor (CDC, 2016). Their bodies begin to appear more similar to that of adults—growth of pubic and underarm hair, and widening of shoulders in boys and hips in girls (CDC, 2016). Girls may also experience their first menstrual cycle and develop breasts, and boys may start to grow facial hair, although boys typically mature later in life than girls (Papalia et al., 2007). As these changes occur at rapid speeds and at rates different from their peers, preadolescents may feel inferior or self-conscious about their changing bodies (CDC, 2016). A combination of age, gender, timing of puberty, and hormonal development increase the heightened emotional reactions characterizing preadolescence (Papalia et al., 2007).

Cognitive

According to Piaget (1969), during late childhood and early adolescence, children begin to have access to formal operational thinking (Piaget, 1969). This new cognitive development is characterized by an increased ability to think hypothetically, consider opposing views, and apply learning from one context to another (CDC, 2016). Evidence suggests that the right hemisphere of the brain, often referred to as the creative and emotional side of the brain, experiences a significant growth spurt during preadolescence (National Institute of Mental Health [NIMH], 2011). Simultaneously, significant growth in the frontal lobe begins to occur, which is responsible for reasoning, regulating emotions, planning, and controlling impulses (Papalia et al., 2007). Thus, while preadolescents begin to practice making rational decisions, they are also flooded with hormones, which make them appear hypersensitive or self-critical (NIMH, 2011). They may make impulsive choices that serve their immediate gratification without analyzing the long-term consequences (Schwartz, 2008).

CPRT Enhances the Parent-Preadolescent Relationship

As is true of CPRT with young children, the primary focus of CPRT for preadolescents is strengthening the parent-preadolescent relationship by equipping parents with basic child-centered play therapy skills. Research indicates that having open communication between parents and preadolescents based on respect, acceptance, and empathy serves as a protective factor to reduce risk-taking behaviors (Coatsworth, Duncan, Greenberg, & Nix, 2010). Because preadolescents experience emotional swings and moodiness, parents might be inclined to become strict and demanding, or disengaged and allow their growing children to have a tremendous amount of freedom (Mbua & Adigeb, 2015). CPRT leaders help parents understand the developmental needs of their children as a way to normalize behavior and to help parents find more appropriate ways of responding to their children (Landreth & Bratton, 2017). The weekly parent-child "special time" and the emphasis on creating family rituals within CPRT are designed to help parents and preadolescents share moments that strengthen the parent-child attachment.

Modifications for CPRT

It is important that CPRT therapists are thoroughly familiar with the CPRT-Preadolescent Model chapter in the second edition of the CPRT text (Landreth & Bratton, 2019). **The CPRT-Preadolescent protocol found on the accompanying Companion Website** details specific adaptations to session outlines, handouts, homework assignments, and toys/materials, as well as developmentally sensitive CCPT responses appropriate for use with preadolescents. Although, theoretically, the CCPT skills are the same regardless of age, the timing and delivery vary to meet the maturational needs of this age group. Because the term *playtime* can be too childish for many preadolescents, the term *special time* is recommended to describe the weekly parent-child time together. Similarly, in addition to or instead of using traditional CPRT toys (Landreth & Bratton, 2019) during *special times*, parents can use more age-appropriate activities including crafts, cooking, baking, outdoor activities such as fishing or hiking, and games that allow for interaction to occur (e.g., puzzles, playing cards). The weekly *special times* can vary depending on the activity and typically ranges from 45 to 90 minutes. Since it is important for preadolescents to develop their independence and have a role in decision making, preadolescents can be involved in deciding the weekly special time activities. Parents can help guide the decision making by providing choices of activities that promote interactions.

References

Baril, M. E., Cromer, A. C., & McHale, S. M. (2007). Process linking adolescent well-being, marital love, and coparenting. *Journal of Family Psychology*, *21*, 645–654.

Bulanda, R. E., & Majumdar, D. (2008). Perceived parent-child relations and adolescent self-esteem. *Journal of Child and Family Studies*, *18*, 203–212.

Center for Disease Control. (2016). *Child development: Middle childhood (9–11 years of age)*. Retrieved from www.cdc.gov/ncbddd/childdevelopment/positiveparenting/middle2.html

Coatsworth, J. D., Duncan, L. O., Greenberg, M. T., & Nix, R. L. (2010). Changing parent's mindfulness, child management skills and relationship quality with their youth: Results from a randomized pilot intervention trial. *Journal of Child and Family Studies*, *19*, 203–217. http://dx.doi.org/10.1007/s10826-009-9304-8

Kretschmer, T., Sentse, M., Kornelis Dijkstra, J., & Veenstra, R. (2014). The interplay between peer rejection and acceptance in preadolescence and early adolescence, Serotonin Transporter gene, and antisocial behavior in late adolescence: The TRIALS study. *Merrill-Palmer Quarterly*, *60*, 193–216.

Landreth, G., & Bratton, S. (2017). *Child Parent Relationship Therapy (CPRT): A 10-session filial therapy model*. New York, NY: Brunner-Routledge.

Lederman, R. P., & Mian, T. S. (2003). The Parent-Adolescent Relationship Education (PARE) program: A curriculum for prevention of STDs and pregnancy in middle school youth. *Behavioral Medicine*, *29*, 33–41. http://dx.doi.org/10.1080/08964280309596173.

Maslow, A. H. (1962). *Towards a psychology of being*. Princeton, NJ: D. Van Nostrand Company.

Mbua, A. P., & Adigeb, A. P. (2015). Parenting styles and adolescents' behaviour in central educational zone of cross river state. *European Scientific Journal*, *11*(22), 354–368.

Meany-Walen, K. K., Carnes Holt, K., Ceballos, P., & Michero, E. (2014). Child parent relationship training: A model for preadolescents. *British Journal of Play Therapy*, *10*, 6–19.

National Institute of Mental Health. (2011). *The teen brain still under construction*. Retrieved from www.nimh.nih.gov/health/publications/the-teen-brain-still-under-construction/teen-brain_141903.pdf

Papalia, D. E., Olds, S. W., & Feldman, R. D. (2007). *Human development* (10th ed.). New York, NY: McGraw-Hill.

Piaget, J. (1969). *The mechanisms of perception*. New York, NY: Basic Books.

Schwartz, K. D. (2008). Adolescent brain development: An oxymoron no longer. *Journal of Youth Ministry*, *6*(2), 85–93.

CPRT ADOPTIVE FAMILIES MODEL

Kristie K. Opiola and Kara Carnes-Holt

CPRT ADOPTIVE FAMILIES MODEL

Kristie K. Opiola and Kara Carnes-Holt

This chapter provides an overview of the protocol for CPRT-Adoptive Families. **The complete CPRT-Adoptive Families Therapist Protocol and Parent Notebook are found on the accompanying Companion Website at www.routledge.com/cw/bratton.** The protocol is designed for use by mental health professionals trained and certified in the CPRT model.

Each year approximately 136,000 children are adopted, adding to the 2 million adopted children in the United States (Kreider & Lofquist, 2014), with 59% adopted from the foster care system and 26% adopted from other countries (The Child Welfare Gateway Center, 2012). Adoption, regardless of age, is a traumatic event (Forbes & Post, 2006; Purvis, Cross, & Sunshine, 2007). Potential adverse experiences and maladjustment risks related to adoptions are present due to long waits for placements, inconsistent caregivers, and associated adverse experiences increase adopted children's risk of interpersonal trauma and insecure attachment (CCAI, 2011; Harris, 2018: Perry & Szalavitz, 2006). Adverse early experiences have damaging effects on children, and the earlier children experience physical or relational harm, the greater the impact on their overall development (Harris, 2018; Perry & Szalavitz, 2006; Purvis et al., 2007).

Thus, in addition to obtaining CPRT certification, facilitators of CPRT-Adoptive Families are strongly encouraged to seek specialized training in the unique needs and challenges of working with adopted and malattached children and their families, including the ability to differentiate adoption-specific and systemic factors that impact adopted children and families.

Rationale for CPRT with Adoptive Families

Children with early relationship trauma struggle to attune and connect with their caregivers, thus adoptive parents often require attachment- and adoption-specific services to help them form a secure attachment with their adoptee (Purvis, Cross, & Pennings, 2009). According to Barth et al. (2005), concerns about the parent-child relationship is the primary motivation that brings adoptive parents to therapy. The foundation philosophy of CPRT is the relationship as the vehicle for change, addressing the core of attachment concerns that many adoptive families experience. The focus of CPRT is on developing a relationship that provides trust, safety, and understanding to promote healthy, secure parent-child attachments and to recreate joy in the adopted child-parent triad (Carnes-Holt & Bratton, 2014; Landreth & Bratton, 2006).

An essential component of CPRT is the parent-child's relational engagement through play. Play allows children to communicate their understanding of their world and express their experiences, needs, and feelings through toys, activities, and materials (Elkind, 2007; Landreth, 2012). CPRT provides adoptive parents the opportunity to learn and implement skills and ways to positively relate and respond to their child that are developmentally responsive and helps parents attune to their adopted child (Opiola & Bratton, 2018). By helping parents take on a therapeutic role, or be an agent of change, parents learn to understand their adopted child's underlying needs, respond more empathically and effectively to their adopted child's behavioral and emotional difficulties, and facilitate their adopted child's ability to self-regulate (Landreth & Bratton, 2004). This one-on-one focused time promotes a secure attachment and is fundamental for children's healthy development and overall well-being.

Adopted Children

Children who experience trauma early in life, such as adoption, tend to be reactive and fearful (von der Kolk, 2005) and can behave in self-defeating ways in order to protect themselves (West, 1992). Adoptees with insecure attachments find creating safety in the parent–child relationship challenging, as they desire closeness with their parent but feel threatened by their parents' attempts to comfort and soothe them during times of distress. Adopted children tend to experience increased fear, sensory-processing issues, difficulty self-regulating, and disorder of memory (Forbes & Post, 2006; Purvis et al., 2007). The child's resulting unpredictable and perplexing behaviors make forming relationships difficult for adoptive parents (Perry & Szalavitz, 2006; Purvis et al., 2007).

Adoptive Parents

Adoptive parents are given the role of mitigating the impact of their children's early relationship experiences; supporting them through recovery, grief, and loss; and facilitating the development of their children's adoptive identities (Brodzinsky, 2013). The journey to healing can be tumultuous due to their children's early experiences. Children with a history of interpersonal trauma, including disruptions in their attachment relationships, tend to misread and misattune to the cues from their caregivers (Opiola & Bratton, 2018; Perry & Szalavitz, 2006). Poor interaction patterns, such as hugging the parent one moment followed immediately by aggression, increase parental stress, and parents' own relationship patterns often connected to early childhood experiences (Purvis et al., 2007) can impact their ability to emotionally respond and attune to their adoptive child (Brodzinsky, 2013).

Modifications for Child-Parent Relationship Therapy for Adoptive Families

It is important that CPRT therapists are thoroughly familiar with the CPRT with adoptive families chapter in the second edition of the CPRT textbook (Landreth & Bratton, 2019). The chapter explores the rationale and argument for modifications from the traditional CPRT model. **The CPRT-Adoptive Families protocol found on the accompanying Companion Website** details specific modifications designed to respond to the unique needs of adoptive families. Modifications include additional sessions; extending length of the sessions; adaptation of assignments; modification to play session location; adjustment to session time structure; inclusion of adoption resources; and extended emotional, educational, and supervision support for parents.

References

Barth, R., Crea, T., John, K., Thoburn, J., Quinton, D., & Daniels, F. (2005). Beyond attachment theory and therapy: Towards sensitive and evidenced-based interventions with foster and adoptive families in distress. *Child and Family Social Work*, *10*, 257–258. doi:10.1111/j.1365-2206.2005.00380.x

Brodzinsky, D. M. (2013). A need to know: Enhancing adoption competence among mental health professionals. In *Policy perspective*. New York, NY: Donaldson Adoption Institute.

Carnes-Holt, K., & Bratton, S. C. (2014). The efficacy of child parent relationship therapy for adopted children with attachment disruptions. *Journal of Counseling & Development*, *92*, 328–337.

Child Welfare Gateway Center. (2012). *Adoption disruption and dissolutions.* Retrieved from www.childwelfare.gov/pubPDFs/s_disrup.pdf

Congressional Coalition on Adoption Institute. (2011). *Facts and statistics.* Retrieved from www.ccainstitute.org/index.php?option=com_content&view=category&layout=blog&id=25&Itemid=43

Elkind, D. (2007). *The power of play: Learning what comes naturally.* Philadelphia, PA: Da Capo Press.

Forbes, H., & Post, B. (2006). *Beyond consequences logic, and control: A love based approach to helping attachment-challenged children with severe behaviors.* Orlando, FL: Beyond Consequences Institute, LLC.

Harris, N. B. (2018). *The deepest well: Healing the long-term effects of childhood adversity.* New York, NY: Houghton Mifflin Harcourt.

Kreider, R. M., & Lofquist, D. A. (2014). *Adopted children and stepchildren: 2010: Population characteristics.* Washington, DC: U.S. Census Bureau.

Landreth, G. L. (2012). *Play therapy: The art of the relationship.* New York, NY: Routledge.

Landreth, G. L., & Bratton, S. C. (2017). *Child parent relationship therapy: A 10-session filial therapy model.* New York, NY: Routledge.

Opiola, K. K., & Bratton, S. C. (2018). The efficacy of child parent relationship therapy (CPRT) for adoptive families: A replication study. *Journal of Counseling & Development, 96*(2), 155–166. doi:10.1002/jcad.12189

Perry, B. D., & Szalavitz, M. (2006). *The boy who was raised as a dog: And other stories from a child psychiatrist's notebook.* Philadelphia, PA: Basic Books.

Purvis, K., Cross, D., & Pennings, J. (2009). Trust-based relational intervention: Interactive principles for adopted children with special social-emotional needs. *The Journal of Humanistic Counseling Education and Development, 48*(1), 3–22.

Purvis, K., Cross, D., & Sunshine, L. (2007). *The connected child: Bring hope and healing to your adoptive family.* New York, NY: McGraw Hill.

von der Kolk, B. A. (2005). *Traumatic stress: The effects of overwhelming experience on mind, body, & society.* New York, NY: Guilford Press.

West, J. (1992). *Child centered play therapy* (2nd ed.). Abingdon, UK: Hodder Education.

CPRT TEACHER MODEL

Child-Teacher Relationship Training (CTRT)

Wendy Pretz Helker and Mary Morrison Bennett

CPRT TEACHER MODEL

Wendy Pretz Helker and Mary Morrison Bennett

This chapter provides an overview of the CTRT protocol for teachers of children in preschool and early elementary school. **The complete CTRT Therapist Protocol and Teacher Notebook are found on the accompanying Companion Website at www.routledge.com/cw/bratton.** The protocol is designed for use by mental health professionals trained and certified in the CPRT model and who have participated in additional training in the CTRT model.

The purpose of Child Teacher Relationship Training (CTRT) is to provide opportunities for teachers to gain a better understanding of children's feelings, experiences, and needs; increase teachers' awareness of ways to respond that build children's confidence and self-esteem; and facilitate the development of more positive emotional relationships with children (Helker & Ray, 2009). The CTRT model is also intended as a useful intervention for children experiencing mental health difficulties in early childhood. Initially teachers are trained to have a special playtime with an individual child in a designated playroom or play area. Later in the training teachers learn to adapt CTRT skills for use with groups of children in the general classroom. Teachers participate in weekly supervision sessions with the CTRT therapist to learn and practice new skills, discuss challenges, ask questions, and gain support and encouragement throughout the training.

Rationale

The catalyst for the development of CTRT was the growing realization that a positive child-teacher relationship can have a multitude of benefits for both the young child and for the professional teacher. An increasing body of research indicates the child-teacher relationship is an important contributing factor in young children's successful academic, social, and emotional development (Howes et al., 2008). The National Association for the Education of Young Children (NAEYC, 2009) position statement on developmentally appropriate practice for early childhood programs proposes that positive, supportive relationships during the earliest years of life appear to be essential not only for cognitive development but also for healthy emotional development. According to the NAEYC (2009), one of the core values underlying all of NAEYC's work is helping children and adults achieve their full potential in the context of relationships based on trust, respect, and positive regard. These core relationship dimensions are central in CTRT training.

A positive child-teacher relationship can impact teachers as well as students. Teachers in positive relationships with children view themselves as competent and successful teachers according to Guerney and Flumen (1970). Children's mental health needs and behavioral difficulties, and teachers' minimal exposure to skills and training designed to meet children's difficulties, may contribute to a challenging relationship between child and teacher. What is especially challenging to teachers is that the children who tend to cause teachers the most discontent may be the very students who most need a positive, high-quality relationship with the teacher.

When a child is exhibiting challenging behaviors in the classroom, it may be due to a mental health issue or need that is not being addressed. According to the most recent U.S. Surgeon General's report on the status of children's mental health (2001), "growing numbers of children are suffering needlessly, because their emotional, behavioral, and developmental needs are not being met" (p. 3). There are several contributing factors to this increasing problem: a shortage of mental health professionals specially trained to work with children; a lack of accessible services; and perhaps most salient, the need for early intervention specifically involving caregivers in the delivery of services. The President's New Freedom Commission on Mental Health (2003) reiterated the need for early intervention and emphasized a need for mental health services to be offered in accessible, low-stigma settings such as schools. CTRT addresses these issues by focusing on core relationship dimensions as seen in the following comments. Teachers who participated in CTRT reported that as a result of CTRT, they "knew how to communicate better with their students, knew more helpful ways to respond to students, were better able to acknowledge students' feelings, felt better able to bond with their students, and understood their students better." After learning the therapeutic skills included in CTRT, teachers also reported feeling more confident in how to work with challenging students. One CTRT participant's powerful comments highlight this idea:

> I believe all teachers should have access to this information. I believe this is especially important in demonstrating how teachers' relationships with their children are so impactful. The limit setting skills, and phrases made a tremendous difference in my classroom. Therefore, I truly think I have become a more competent teacher.

Modifications of CPRT for CTRT

Although CTRT is consistent with the philosophy, content, and process of CPRT, the model required modifications to fit the needs of the teacher-student relationship and the application of training in the school environment. As in CPRT, teachers are taught the basic principles, attitudes, and skills of CCPT to use initially with a child of focus from their classroom and then later to generalize for use with all students in their class.

The full CTRT protocol for therapists and handouts for teachers are included on the accompanying Companion Website. The following is an overview of how CTRT is organized over the 20-week period. The structure and format of CTRT is designed to accommodate teachers' schedules and make use of beginning of the year in-service days for the initial intensive training.

Phase I CTRT-Skills Outline

2-Day Intensive CTRT Training (covers content of CTRT Sessions 1–4)

- Overview of CTRT Philosophy
- Essential Concepts of Training
- Reflective Responding
- Play Session Dos and Don'ts
- Play Session Toys and Materials Demonstration
- Limit Setting

CTRT Sessions 5–10 held during weekly CTRT sessions

- Supervision of CTRT Playtime Skills
- Choice Giving
- Esteem Building
- Encouragement

Phase II CTRT Classroom Skills Outline

Sessions 11–20

- Objectives and Structure of CTRT Time
- Basic and Advanced Group Responding Skills
- Advanced Choice Giving for Teachers
- Advanced Limit Setting, ACT for the Classroom
- Anger and Aggression in Children
- Trouble Shooting in the Classroom

Phase III Observation and Accountability

The final phase of CTRT includes unscheduled observation of the teachers in the general classroom 3 or 4 weeks after the conclusion of the CTRT training using the CTRT-Skills Checklist (CTRT-SC). The CTRT-Skills Checklist (Helker, 2006) can be found in the CTRT protocol/manual on the accompanying Companion Website. The purpose of the observations is to determine to what degree teachers learned and integrated relationship-building skills in the classroom and as a data collection tool for use in evaluation of CTRT.

References

Guerney, B. G., Jr., & Flumen, A. B. (1970). Teachers as psychotherapeutic agents for withdrawn children. *Journal of School Psychology, 8*, 107–113.

Helker, W. P. (2006). *The impact of child teacher relationship training on teachers' and aides use of relationship -building skills and the effect on student classroom behavior* (Order No. 3254192). Available from ProQuest Dissertations & Theses Global. (305295221). Retrieved from http://libproxy.txstate.edu/login?url=http://search.proquest.com/docview/305295221?accountid=5683

Helker, W. P., & Ray, D. C. (2009). Impact of child teacher relationship training on teachers' and aides' use of relationship-building skills and the effects on student classroom behavior. *International Journal of Play Therapy, 18*(4), 70–83.

Howes, C., Burchinal, M., Pianta, R., Bryant, D., Early, D., Clifford, R., & Barbarin, O. (2008). Ready to learn? Children's pre-academic achievement in pre-kindergarten programs. *Early Childhood Research Quarterly, 23*(1), 27–50.

National Association for the Education of Young Children. (2009). *Developmentally appropriate practice in early childhood programs serving children from birth through age 8*. Retrieved from www.naeyc.org/files/naeyc/file/positions/PSDAP.pdf

New Freedom Commission on Mental Health. (2003). *Achieving the promise: Transforming mental health care in America*. Final report (DHHS Publication No. SMA-03-3832). Rockville, MD: U.S. Department of Health and Human Services.

United States Public Health Service. (2001). *Report of the surgeon general's conference on children's mental health: A national agenda*. US Government—Public Health Service: Washington, DC.

CHILD-PARENT-RELATIONSHIP (C-P-R) TRAINING AGES 3–10 PARENT NOTEBOOK

Parent Handouts, Notes, and Homework Sessions 1–10

Using the Parent Notebook

Therapists download and print copies of the *Parent Notebook – Ages 3–10* from the Companion Website found at www.routledge.com/cw/bratton. Therapists are expected to be thoroughly familiar with the downloaded *Parent Notebook* organization and pagination. *Note: The Parent Notebooks for each of the new adapted CPRT protocols (Toddler, Preadolescent, and Adoptive Families) and the Teacher Notebook for the Student-Teacher model) are available on the Companion Website.*

The *Parent Notebook for Ages 3–10* includes all of the printed materials that parents will need to complete CPRT training. For ease of duplication and to ensure correct pagination, the *Parent Notebook* is intended to be printed from the Companion Website, rather than copied from this manual. The Companion Website version of the *Parent Notebook for Ages 3–10* is formatted for two-sided printing with blank pages inserted where needed so that each new session begins on odd numbered page. We suggest organizing the notebook into a three-brad pocket folder or small three-ring binder with 1–10 tabs to designate the 10 sessions. Other useful strategies for the organization of training materials include printing the most used handouts, *Play Session Dos and Don'ts, Play Session Procedures Checklist*, and *CPRT Cliff Notes* on different colors of paper or using tabs to provide an easy method for parents to locate them in their notebooks.

Handouts in the *Parent Notebook* are organized by the CPRT training session in which they are typically used. Some flexibility in presenting materials is allowed, depending on the needs of a particular group of parents. Appendix A contains additional resources that the therapist can provide to parents. Supplemental skill practice worksheets for parents are also included in Appendix D. Although these supplemental worksheets are provided as additional practice for CPRT skills that a particular group of parents may be struggling to put into practice, the therapist is cautioned to avoid overwhelming parents with too much information or homework. Again, it is expected that the therapist will **exercise clinical judgment** in determining when and if to use supplemental materials.

Please note that permission to copy the materials is granted to the therapist in conjunction with the purchase of the *CPRT Treatment Manual*. The copyright statement on the cover page of the *Parent Notebook* should be printed out and included in the notebook handed out to parents.

CHILD-PARENT-RELATIONSHIP (C-P-R) TRAINING
Parent Notes and Homework—Session 1

👍 RULES OF THUMB TO REMEMBER:

1. **"Focus on the donut, not the hole!"** Focus on the Relationship, NOT the Problem.
2. **"Be a thermostat, not a thermometer."** Learn to RESPOND (reflect) rather than REACT.

   Remember: The best way to calm your child is to first calm and center yourself.
3. **"What's most important may not be what you do, but what you do after what you have done!"** We all make mistakes, but we can recover. It is how we handle our mistakes that makes the difference.

Reflective Responding:

A way of following, rather than leading.

Reflect behaviors, thoughts, needs/wishes, and feelings (without asking questions).

Helps you understand your child and helps your child feel understood.

"Be-With" Attitudes Convey:	Not:
I am here; I hear you.	I always agree.
I understand.	I must make you happy.
I care.	I will solve your problems.

Notes: (use back for additional notes)

____

____

____

Homework Assignments:

- ☐ Practice reflective responding (complete *Feeling Response: Homework Worksheet* and bring next week).
- ☐ Notice one physical characteristic about your child you haven't seen before.

  ____
- ☐ Bring your favorite, heart-tugging picture of your child of focus.
- ☐ Practice giving a 30-second Burst of Attention. If you are on the telephone, say, "Can you hold for 30 seconds? I'll be right back." Put the phone aside, bend down, and give your child undivided, focused attention for 30 seconds; then say, "I have to finish talking to _______________." Stand back up and continue talking with your friend.

CHILD-PARENT-RELATIONSHIP (C-P-R) TRAINING
Feelings Response: In-Class Practice Worksheet—Session 1

Directions: (1) Look into child's eyes for clue to feeling. (2) After you've decided what child is feeling, put the feeling word into a short response, generally beginning with <u>you</u>, "you seem sad" or "you're really mad at me right now." (3) Your facial expression and tone of voice should match your child's (empathy is conveyed more through non-verbals than verbals).

Child: Oscar is telling you all the things he's going to show his older cousin, Sophia, this weekend.

Child Felt: ________________________________
Parent Response: ____________________________

Child: Serena gets in the car after school and tells you that Bert, the class pet hamster, died—and then tells you about how she was in charge of feeding Bert last week and how he would look at her and then get on his wheel and run.

Child Felt: ________________________________
Parent Response: ____________________________

Child: Andre was playing with his friend, Harry, when Harry grabbed Andre's fire truck and wouldn't give it back. Andre tried to get it back and the ladder broke off. Andre comes to you crying and tells you what happened and that it's all Harry's fault.

Child Felt: ________________________________
Parent Response: ____________________________.

Child: Zara was playing in the garage while you were cleaning it out, when a big box of books falls off the shelf and hits the floor behind her. She jumps up and runs over to you.

Child Felt: ________________________________
<u>(depends on child's facial expression)</u>
Parent Response: ____________________________!

CHILD-PARENT-RELATIONSHIP (C-P-R) TRAINING
Feelings Response: Homework Worksheet—Session 1

Directions: (1) Look into child's eyes for clue to feeling. (2) After you've decided what child is feeling, put the feeling word into a short response, generally beginning with you, "you seem sad" or "you're really mad at me right now." (3) Remember the importance of your facial expression and tone of voice matching child's (empathy is conveyed more through non-verbals than verbals).

Child: (what happened/what child did or said)

____

____

____

Child Felt: ______________________________

Parent Response: ______________________________

____

____

Alternate Response (if needed):

____

____

Child: (what happened/what child did or said)

____

____

____

Child Felt: ______________________________

Parent Response: ______________________________

____

____

Alternate Response (if needed):

____

____

Child: (what happened/what child did or said)

____

____

____

Child Felt: ______________________________

Parent Response: ______________________________

____

____

Alternate Response (if needed):

____

____

Child: (what happened/what child did or said)

____

____

____

Child Felt: ______________________________

Parent Response: ______________________________

____

____

Alternate Response (if needed):

____

____

CHILD-PARENT-RELATIONSHIP (C-P-R) TRAINING
What Is It and How Can It Help?

What Is It?

Child-Parent-Relationship (C-P-R) Training is a special 10-session parent training program to help strengthen the relationship between a parent and a child by using 30-minute playtimes once a week. Play is the most natural way children communicate. Toys are like words for children and play is their language. Adults talk about their experiences, thoughts, and feelings. Children use toys to explore their experiences and express what they think and how they feel. Therefore, parents are taught to have special structured 30-minute playtimes with their child using a kit of carefully selected toys in their own home. Parents learn how to respond empathically to their child's feelings, build their child's self-esteem, help their child learn self-control and self-responsibility, and set therapeutic limits during these special playtimes.

For 30 minutes each week, the child is the center of the parent's universe. In this special playtime, the parent creates an accepting relationship in which a child feels completely safe to express himself through his play—fears, likes, dislikes, wishes, anger, loneliness, joy, or feelings of failure. This is not a typical playtime. It is a special playtime in which the child leads and the parent follows. In this special relationship, there are no:

- reprimands
- put-downs
- evaluations
- requirements (to draw pictures a certain way, etc.)
- judgments (about the child or his play as being good or bad, right or wrong)

How Can It Help My Child?

In the special playtimes, you will build a different kind of relationship with your child, and your child will discover that she is capable, important, understood, and accepted as she is. When children experience a play relationship in which they feel accepted, understood, and cared for, they play out many of their problems and, in the process, release tensions, feelings, and burdens. Your child will then feel better about herself and will be able to discover her own strengths and assume greater self-responsibility as she takes charge of play situations.

How your child feels about herself will make a significant difference in her behavior. In the special playtimes where you learn to focus on your child rather than your child's problem, your child will begin to react differently, because how your child behaves, how she thinks, and how she performs in school are directly related to how she feels about herself. When your child feels better about herself, she will behave in more self-enhancing ways rather than self-defeating ways.

CHILD-PARENT-RELATIONSHIP (C-P-R) TRAINING
Parent Notes and Homework—Session 2

RULES OF THUMB TO REMEMBER:

1. **"The parent's toes should follow his/her nose."**
2. **"You can't give away that which you don't possess."** You can't extend patience and acceptance to your child if you can't first offer it to yourself. As your child's most significant caregiver, you are asked to give so much of yourself, often when you simply don't have the resources within you to meet the demands of parenting.

Remember the analogy of the oxygen mask on an airplane!

____

Focus on the "Be-With" Attitudes
I'm here—I hear you—I understand—I care—I delight in you!

Notes: (use back for additional notes)

____

____

____

____

____

____

____

Homework Assignments:

☐ Priority—Collect toys on *Toy Checklist for Play Sessions.*

☐ Select a consistent time and an uninterrupted place in the home suitable for the play sessions and report back next week—whatever room you feel offers the fewest distractions to the child and the greatest freedom from worry about breaking things or making a mess. Set aside a regular time in advance that is best for you and your child. This time is to be undisturbed—no phone calls or interruptions by other children.

Time ________________ *Place* ______________________________________

☐ Review *Basic Principles of Play Sessions* handout

☐ Additional Assignment:

CHILD-PARENT-RELATIONSHIP (C-P-R) TRAINING
Toy Checklist for Play Sessions—Session 2

Note: Obtain sturdy cardboard box with lid or plastic container with lid to store toys (box that copier paper comes in is ideal—the deep lid becomes a dollhouse). Use an old blanket to arrange toys on and to serve as a boundary for the play area.

Real-Life Toys (also promote imaginative play)

- ☐ Small baby doll: *should not be anything "special"; can be extra one that child does not play with anymore*
- ☐ Baby bottle: *real one so it can be used by the child to put a drink in during the session*
- ☐ Doctor kit (with stethoscope): *add three Band-Aids for each session (add disposable gloves/Ace bandage, if you have)*
- ☐ Toy phones: *recommend getting two in order to communicate: one cell, one regular*
- ☐ Doll family: *bendable mother, father, brother, sister, baby, and so forth (representative of your family)*
- ☐ Play money: *bills and coins; credit card is optional*
- ☐ Couple of domestic and wild animals: *if you don't have doll family, you can substitute an animal family (e.g., horse, cow family)*
- ☐ Car/truck: *one to two small ones (could make specific to child's needs, e.g., an ambulance)*
- ☐ Kitchen dishes: *couple of plastic dishes, cups, and eating utensils*

Optional

- ☐ Small dollhouse: *use deep lid of box the toys are stored in—draw room divisions, windows, doors, and so forth inside of lid*
- ☐ Puppets: *one aggressive, one gentle; can be homemade or purchased (animal-shaped cooking mittens, etc.)*
- ☐ Doll furniture: *for a bedroom, bathroom, and kitchen*
- ☐ Dress up: *hand mirror, bandana, scarf; small items you already have around the house*

Acting-Out Aggressive Toys (also promote imaginative play)

- ☐ Dart guns with a couple of darts and a target: *parent needs to know how to operate*
- ☐ Rubber knife: *small, bendable, army type*
- ☐ Rope: *prefer soft rope (can cut the ends off jump rope)*
- ☐ Aggressive animal: (*e.g., snake, shark, lion, dinosaurs—strongly suggest hollow shark!*)
- ☐ Small toy soldiers (12-15): *two different colors to specify two teams or good guys/bad guys*
- ☐ Inflatable bop bag (Bobo *clown style preferable*)
- ☐ Mask: *Lone Ranger type*
- ☐ Toy handcuffs with a key

Toys for Creative/Emotional Expression

- ☐ Play-Doh: *suggest a cookie sheet or plastic placemat to put Play-Doh on to contain mess—also serves as a flat surface for drawing*
- ☐ Crayons: *eight colors, break some and peel paper off (markers are optional for older children but messier)*
- ☐ Plain paper: *provide a few pieces of new paper for each session*
- ☐ Scissors: *not pointed, but that cut well (e.g., child Fiskarsµ)*
- ☐ Transparent tape: *remember, child can use up all of this, so buy several of smaller size*
- ☐ Egg carton, styrofoam cup/bowl: *for destroying, breaking, or coloring*
- ☐ Ring toss game
- ☐ Soft foam ball
- ☐ Small musical instrument (preferably two)

Optional

- ☐ Selection of arts/crafts materials in a ziplock bag (*e.g., colored construction paper, glue, yarn, buttons, beads, scraps of fabrics, raw noodles, etc.—much of this depends on age of child*)
- ☐ Tinkertoys/small assortment of building blocks
- ☐ Binoculars
- ☐ Magic Wand
- ☐ Two balloons (per play session)

***Reminder:** Toys need not be new or expensive. Avoid selecting more toys than will fit in a box—toys should be small. In some cases, additional toys can be added based on child's need and with therapist approval. If unable to get every toy before first play session, obtain several from each category—ask therapist for help in prioritizing.*

Note: Unwrap any new toys or take out of box before play session. Toys should look inviting.

Good Toy Hunting Places: garage sales, friends/relatives, "dollar" stores

CHILD-PARENT-RELATIONSHIP (C-P-R) TRAINING
Basic Principles of Play Sessions—Session 2

Basic Principles for Play Sessions:

1. The parent sets the stage by structuring an atmosphere in which the **child feels free** to determine how he will use the time during the 30-minute play session. The **child leads** the play and the **parent follows.** The parent follows the child's lead by showing keen interest and carefully observing the child's play, **without making suggestions or asking questions**, and by actively joining in the play when invited by the child. For 30 minutes, you (parent) are "dumb" and don't have the answers; it is up to your child to make his own decisions and find his own solutions. Your child is the expert.
2. The parent's major task is to empathize with the child: to understand the child's thoughts, feelings, and intent expressed in play by working hard to **see and experience the child's play through the child's eyes.** This task is operationalized by conveying the "Be-With" Attitudes below.
3. The parent is then to **communicate this understanding to the child** by (a) verbally describing what the child is doing/playing, (b) verbally reflecting what the child is saying, and (c) most importantly, by verbally reflecting the feelings that the child is actively experiencing through his play.
4. The parent is to be clear and firm about the few "limits" that are placed on the child's behavior. Limits are stated in a way that give the child responsibility for his actions and behaviors—helping to foster self-control. Limits to be set are time limits, not breaking toys or damaging items in the play area, and not physically hurting self or parent. **Limits are to be stated only when needed**, but applied consistently across sessions. (Specific examples of when and how to set limits will be taught over the next several weeks; you will also have lots of opportunities to practice this very important skill.)

"Be-With" Attitudes:

Your intent in your actions, presence, and responses is what is most important and should convey to your child:

"I am here—I hear you—I understand—I care—I delight in you!"

Goals of the Play Sessions:

1. To allow the child—through the medium of play—to communicate thoughts, needs, and feelings to his parent, and for the parent to communicate that understanding back to the child.
2. To help the child experience more positive feelings of self-respect, self-worth, confidence, and competence—through feeling accepted, understood, and valued—and ultimately develop self-control, responsibility for actions, and learn to get needs met in appropriate ways.
3. To strengthen the parent-child relationship and foster a sense of trust, security, and closeness for both parent and child.
4. To increase the level of playfulness and enjoyment between parent and child. Enjoy 30 minutes of time together!

CHILD-PARENT-RELATIONSHIP (C-P-R) TRAINING
Parent Notes and Homework—Session 3

RULE OF THUMB TO REMEMBER:

"Be a thermostat, not a thermometer."

Reflecting/responding to your child's thoughts, feelings, and needs creates an atmosphere of understanding and acceptance for your child and helps prevent problems.

During the 30-minute play session, you are to be a thermostat for your child.

Basic Limit Setting:

Focus on Communicate the limit and Target an alternative

If child picks up the gun and aims it at you:

"Jamal, I know you'd like to shoot the gun at me, but I'm not for shooting. You can choose to shoot at that" (point at something acceptable)."

If child starts to smash Play Doh on the floor:

"Lucy, I know you're really having fun with that, but the Play-Doh is not for the floor/carpet. You can choose to smash it on the tray or a piece of paper."

Notes: (use back for additional notes)

____

____

____

____

____

Note: You may wish to explain to your child that you are having these special playtimes with him or her because "I am going to this special play class to learn some special ways to play with you!"

Homework Assignments:

- ☐ Complete play session toy kit—get blanket and other materials (see *Photograph of Toys Set Up for Play Session* in handouts) and confirm that the time and place you chose will work. Make arrangements for other children.
- ☐ *Explain to your child that you are having these special playtimes with him or her because "I am going to this special play class to learn some special ways to play with you!"* Then, give your child an appointment card (display where child can see the card: suggest taping card to mirror in the bathroom where child brushes teeth).
- ☐ Make "Special Playtime—Do Not Disturb" sign with child 1 to 3 days ahead (depending on child's age). The younger the child, the closer to the time of play session.
- ☐ Read over handouts prior to play session:
  - *Play Session Procedures Checklist*
  - *Play Session Dos & Don'ts*
- ☐ Play sessions begin at home this week—arrange to video-record your session and make notes about problems or questions you have about your sessions.

____ I will bring my video next week (if video-recording at clinic: my appt. day/time ____).

CHILD-PARENT-RELATIONSHIP (C-P-R) TRAINING
Play Session Procedures Checklist—Session 3

Depending on age of child, may need to remind him or her: "Today is the day for our special playtime!"

A. Prior to Session (Remember to "Set the Stage")

- ☐ Make arrangements for other family members (so that there will be no interruptions).
- ☐ Prepare a snack or activity for after the play session (see item D. below)
- ☐ Set up toys on old quilt—keep toy placement predictable.
- ☐ Have a clock visible in the room (or wear a watch).
- ☐ Put pets outside or in another room.
- ☐ Let the child use the bathroom prior to the play session.
- ☐ Switch on video recorder.

B. Beginning the Session

- ☐ Child and Parent: Hang "Do Not Disturb" sign (can also "unplug" phone if there is one in play session area). *Message to child: "This is so important that <u>No One</u> is allowed to interrupt this time together."*
- ☐ Tell Child: "*We will have 30 minutes of special playtime, and you can play with the toys in lots of the ways you want to.*"
  (Voice needs to convey that parent is looking forward to this time with child.)
- ☐ <u>From this point on, let the child lead.</u>

C. During the Session

- ☐ Sit on the same level as child, close enough to show interest but allowing enough space for child to move freely.
- ☐ Focus your eyes, ears, and body fully on child. (*Toes Follow Nose!*) Conveys full attention!
- ☐ Your voice should mostly be gentle and caring, but vary with the intensity and affect of child's play.
- ☐ Allow the child to identify the toys. (To promote make-believe play [e.g., what looks like a car to you might be a spaceship to your child], try to use nonspecific words ["this," "that," "it"] if child hasn't named toy.)
- ☐ Play actively with the child, if the child requests your participation.
- ☐ Verbally reflect what you see and hear (child's play/activity, thoughts, feelings).
- ☐ Set limits on behaviors that make you feel uncomfortable.
- ☐ Give 5-minute advance notice for session's end and then a 1-minute notice.
  ("Anika, we have 5 minutes left in our special playtime.")

D. Ending the Session

- ☐ At 30 minutes, <u>stand</u> and announce, **"Our playtime is over for today."** Do not exceed time limit by more than 2 to 3 minutes.
- ☐ Parent does the cleaning up. If child chooses, child may help. (If child continues to play while "cleaning," set limit below.)
- ☐ <u>If child has difficulty leaving:</u>
  - Open the door or begin to put away toys.
  - Reflect child's feelings about not wanting to leave, but calmly and firmly restate that the playtime is over. (Restate limit as many times as needed—the goal is for child to be able to stop herself.)
    "I know you would like to stay and play with the toys, but our special playtime is over for today."
  - Adding a statement that gives child something to look forward to helps child see that, although she cannot continue to play with the special toys, there is something else she can do that is also enjoyable. For example:
    1. **"You can play with the toys (or specific toy) next week during our special playtime."**
    2. **"It's time for snack; would you like grapes or cherries today?"**
    3. **"We can go outside and play on the trampoline."**

<u>Note</u>: Patience is the order of the day when helping child to leave—OK to repeat limit calmly several times to allow child to struggle with leaving on her own. (Key is showing empathy and understanding in your voice tone and facial expressions as you state the limit.) Younger children may need more time to "hear" limit and respond.

Never use Special Playtime as a reward or consequence—no matter the child's behavior that day!

CHILD-PARENT-RELATIONSHIP (C-P-R) TRAINING
Play Session Dos & Don'ts—Session 3

Parents: *Your major task is to show genuine and intentional interest in your child's play. You communicate your interest in, and understanding of, your child's thoughts, feelings, and behavior through your words, actions, and undivided focus on your child.*

Do:

1. **Do set the stage. (Structure for Success!)**
   - Prepare play area ahead of time (old blanket can be used to establish a visual boundary of the play area, as well as provide protection for flooring; a cookie sheet under the arts/crafts materials provides a hard surface for Play-Doh, drawing, and gluing and provides ease of clean up).
   - Display the toys in a consistent manner around the perimeter of the play area.
   - Convey *freedom* as you introduce your special playtime to your child: ***"During our special playtime, you can play with the toys in lots of the ways you'd like to."***
   - Allow your child to lead by returning responsibility to your child using responses, such as *"That's up to you," "You can decide,"* or *"That can be whatever you want it to be."*
2. **Do let your child lead.**
   - Allowing your child to lead during the playtime helps you to better understand your child's world and what your child needs from you.
   - Communicate your willingness to follow your child's lead through your responses: *"Show me what you want me to do," "You want me to put that on," "Hmmm. . .," "* or "I wonder . . ."
   - Use whisper technique (co-conspirators) when child wants you to play a role: *"What should I say?" or "What happens next?"* (Modify responses for older kids: use conspiratorial tone, "What happens now?" "What kind of teacher am I?" etc.)
3. **Do join in your child's play actively and playfully, *as a follower*.**
   - Convey your willingness to follow your child's lead through your responses and your actions, by **actively** joining in the play (child is the director, parent is the actor) using responses, such as "So I'm supposed to be the teacher," "You want me to be the robber, and I'm supposed to wear the black mask," "Now I'm supposed to pretend I'm locked up in jail, until you say I can get out," or "You want me to stack these just as high as yours."
   - You can also use the whisper technique described above.
4. **Do verbally track the child's play** (describe what you see).
   - Verbally tracking your child's play is a way of letting your child know that you are paying close attention and that you are interested and involved.
   - Use observational responses, such as *"You're filling that all the way to the top," "You've decided you want to paint next,"* or *"You've got 'em all lined up just how you want them."*
5. **Do reflect your child's feelings.**
   - Verbally reflecting children's feelings helps them feel understood and communicates your acceptance of their feelings and needs.
   - Use reflective responses, such as *"You're proud of your picture," "That kinda surprised you," "You really like how that feels on your hands," "You really wish that we could play longer," "You don't like the way that turned out,"* or *"You sound disappointed." (Hint: Look closely at your child's face to better identify how your child is feeling.)*
6. **Do set firm and consistent limits.**
   - Consistent limits create a structure for a safe and predictable environment for children.
   - Children should never be permitted to hurt themselves or you.
   - Limit setting provides an opportunity for your child to develop self-control and self-responsibility.
   - Using a calm, patient, yet firm voice, say, "I know you're having fun, but *the carpet's not for putting Play-Doh on; you can play with it on the tray"* or *"I know you'd like to shoot the gun at me, but I'm not for shooting. You can choose to shoot at that"* (point to something acceptable).
7. **Do salute the child's power and encourage effort.**
   - Verbally recognizing and encouraging your child's effort builds self-esteem and confidence and promotes self-motivation.
   - Use self-esteem-building responses, such as *"You worked hard on that!" "You did it!" "You figured it out!" "You've got a plan for how you're gonna set those up," "You know just how you want that to be,"* or *"Sounds like you know lots about how to take care of babies."*
8. **Do be verbally active.**
   - Being verbally active communicates to your child that you are interested and involved in her play. If you are silent, your child will feel watched.
   - *Note: Empathic grunts—"Hmm . . ." and so forth—also convey interest and involvement, when you are unsure of how to respond.*

Don't:

1. Don't *criticize* any behavior.
2. Don't praise the child.
3. Don't ask leading questions.
4. Don't allow external interruptions of the session.
5. Don't give information or teach.
6. Don't preach.
7. Don't initiate new activities.
8. Don't be passive or quiet.

(Don'ts 1-7 are taken from Guerney, 1972.)

Remember the "Be-With" Attitudes: Your intent in your responses is what is most important. Convey to your child:

"I am here—I hear you—I understand—I care."

Reminder: These play session skills (the new skills you are applying) are relatively meaningless if applied mechanically and not as an attempt to be genuinely empathic and truly understanding of your child. **Your Intent and Attitude Are More Important Than Your Words!**

CHILD-PARENT-RELATIONSHIP (C-P-R) TRAINING
Photograph of Toys Set Up for Play Session—Session 3

CHILD-PARENT-RELATIONSHIP (C-P-R) TRAINING
Parent Notes and Homework—Session 4

✍ RULES OF THUMB TO REMEMBER:

1. **"When a child is drowning, don't try to teach her to swim."** When a child is feeling upset or out of control, that is not the moment to impart a rule or teach a lesson.

   Your job is to "save your child" when he/she is drowning in emotions. You can help calm your child and co-regulate his/her feelings and behavior by calmly conveying your understanding and acceptance through your words and actions.
2. **"During play sessions, limits are not needed until they are needed!"**

Basic Limit Setting:

Start by saying child's name: "Sarah,"
Acknowledge the Feeling: "I know you'd like to shoot the dart gun at me. . . " (with empathy)
Communicate the Limit: "but I'm not for shooting."
Target acceptable Alternative: You *can choose to shoot at that" (point at something acceptable).*

Notes: (use back for additional notes)

____

____

____

____

____

____

Homework Assignments:

☐ Complete *Limit Setting: A-C-T Practice Worksheet.*
☐ Read over handouts prior to play session:
- *Limit Setting: A-C-T Before It's Too Late!*
- *CPRT Cliff Notes*
- *Play Session Dos & Don'ts*
- *Play Session Procedures Checklist*

☐ Conduct play session (same time and place):
- Complete *Play Session Notes.*
- Notice one feeling in yourself during your play session this week.

____ ***I will bring my video next week (if video-recording at clinic: my appt. day/time ____).***

CHILD-PARENT-RELATIONSHIP (C-P-R) TRAINING
Limit Setting: A-C-T Before It's Too Late!—Session 4

Acknowledge the feeling

Communicate the limit

Target alternatives

Three Step A-C-T Method of Limit Setting:

Scenario: Damian has been pretending that the bop bag is a bad guy and shooting him with the dart gun; he looks over at you and aims the dart gun at you, then laughs and says, "Now, you're one of the bad guys, too!"

1. Acknowledge your child's feeling or desire (*your voice must convey empathy and understanding*).
   "Damian, I know that you think that it would be fun to shoot me, too . . ."
   Child learns that his feelings, desires, and wishes are valid and accepted by parent (but not all behavior); just empathically reflecting your child's feeling often defuses the intensity of the feeling or need.
2. Communicate the limit (be specific and clear—and brief).
   "but I'm not for shooting."
3. Target acceptable alternatives (provide one or more choices, depending on age of child).
   "You can pretend that the doll is one of the bad guys (pointing at the doll) and shoot at it."
   The goal is to provide your child with an acceptable outlet for expressing the feeling or the original action, while giving him an opportunity to exercise self-control. Note: Pointing helps redirect child's attention.

When to Set Limits?

RULE OF THUMB: "During play sessions, limits are not needed until they are needed!" Limits are set only when the need arises, and for four basic reasons:

- To protect child from hurting himself or parent.
- To protect valuable property.
- To maintain parent's acceptance of child.
- To provide consistency in the play session by limiting child and toys to play area and ending on time.

Before setting a limit in a play session, ask yourself:

- "Is this limit necessary?"
- "Can I consistently enforce this limit?"
- "If I don't' set a limit on this behavior, can I consistently allow this behavior and accept my child?"

Avoid conducting play sessions in areas of the house that require too many limits. Limits set during play sessions should allow for greater freedom of expression than would normally be allowed. The fewer the limits, the easier it is for you to be consistent—**consistency is very important**. Determine a few limits ahead of time (practice A-C-T): no hitting or shooting at parent, no Play-Doh on carpet, no purposefully breaking toys, and so forth. *Hint: Children really do understand that playtimes are "special" and that the rules are different—they will not expect the same level of permissiveness during the rest of the week.*

How to Set Limits?

Limits are not punitive and should be stated firmly, but calmly and matter-of-factly. After empathically acknowledging your child's feeling or desire (very important step), you state, "The Play-Doh is not for throwing at the table," just like you would state, "The sky is blue." Don't try to force your child to obey the limit. Remember to provide an acceptable alternative. In this method, it really is up to the child to decide to accept or break the limit; however, **it is your job, as the parent, to consistently enforce the limit**. Remember to be patient. This is a new experience for your child. It may be necessary to repeat the limit one to two times to allow your child to bring self under control.

Why Establish Consistent Limits?

Providing children with consistent limits helps them feel safe and secure. This method of limiting children's behavior teaches them self-control and responsibility for their own behavior by allowing them to experience the consequences of their choices and decisions. Limits set in play sessions help children practice self-control and begin to learn to stop themselves in the real world.

CONSISTENT LIMITS → PREDICTABLE, SAFE ENVIRONMENT → SENSE OF SECURITY

CHILD-PARENT-RELATIONSHIP (C-P-R) TRAINING
Limit Setting: A-C-T Practice Worksheet—Session 4

Acknowledge the feeling

Communicate the limit

Target alternatives

Example # 1

Gabrielle is using glue to make a creation during playtime. In attempt to be funny, she puts the glue bottle over your head as if she will squeeze glue in your hair.

A **"Gabrielle, I know that you think that would be funny,"**

C **"but my hair is not for glue."**

T **"You can squeeze glue *all* over on the paper."** (Your voice can match her playfulness.)

Example # 2

The play session time is up, and you have stated the limit two times. Your child becomes angry because you won't give in and let him play longer; he begins to hit you. Hitting is not allowed, so go immediately to second step of A-C-T, then follow with all three steps of A-CT method of limit setting.

C (firmly) **"Eduardo, I'm not for hitting."**

A (empathically) **"I know you're mad/frustrated,"**

C (firmly) **"but people aren't for hitting."**

T (neutral tone) **"You can hit the bop bag or hit this pillow." (pointing to the bop bag or pillow)**

Practice:

1. In the midst of a playful sword fight between you and your child, your child hits your face with the foam sword.

   A *[Child's name], I know you are* ______________________________.

   C *But my face is not* ______________________________.

   T *You can choose to* ______________ *(as you point to* ______________*)*.

2. After 15 minutes of the play session, your child announces that she wants to leave and go upstairs to play a video game.

   A I know you ______________________________.

   C *but* ______________________________.

   T Then *you can* ______________________________.

Child-Parent-Relationship (C-P-R) Training
Page 2—Limit Setting: A-C-T Practice Worksheet—Session 4

3. Your child wants to play doctor and asks you to be the patient. Your child asks you to pull up your shirt so that she/he can listen to your heart.

   A *[Child's name], I know you want* ______________________________.

   C *But* ______________________________.

   T *You can* ______________________________.

4. Describe a situation in which you think you might need to set a limit during the play session.

   Situation: ______________________________

   ____

   A ______________________________

   C ______________________________

   T ______________________________

CHILD-PARENT-RELATIONSHIP (C-P-R) TRAINING
Cliff Notes for Parents—Session 4

Remember:

1. Essential "Be-With" Attitudes: I'm here—I hear you—I understand—I care—I delight in you!
2. Importance of nonverbals (face and voice congruent with words; toes follow nose; lean towards child)
3. Avoid asking questions; instead make reflections/statements (trust your experience/instinct; sometimes you aren't sure, but child will correct you if you are wrong)
4. Often helpful to start reflection with: **You/You're . . .**" to give child credit for actions/intent.
5. Other reflections that can be useful in conveying (a) acceptance of the child, (b) freedom of the playtime, c) belief that the child will take her play in the direction she needs, (d) belief that the child is inherently worthy of being valued and prized, and (e) trust that the child is capable of self-direction and problem solving:

   "You're wondering. . ."
   "In here, you can decide."
   "It can be whatever you want it to be."
   "That's up to you."
   "Hmm - I wonder. . . . "
   "Show me what you want me to do."
   "What should I say/do; What happens next?"
   (stage whisper - child is director and you are the actor, with no script)
   "You know just what you want to do."
   "You decided to. . ."
   "You did it" (important that your affect matches child)
   "You got that just the way you wanted it to go."
   "You figured that out."
   "You're working hard to get that off."
   "You're determined to figure that out."
   "You look happy, proud, sad, etc . . . about that."

6. Therapeutic Limit Setting: conveys <u>your empathic understanding of the child's intent/desire</u> and provides the child with the opportunity to bring self under control. **Remember: A-C-T**

   *"Isabella, **(A)** I know you'd like to shoot the picture, **(C)** but, the picture isn't for shooting. **(T)** You can shoot the dart at the wall (pointing to wall)"*

   *"Isabella, **(A)** You'd like to play with the playdoh on the carpet, **(C)** but the playdoh is for staying on the tray" (sometimes you don't need a "T")*

   *"Isabella, **(A)** You'd really like to play longer, but **(C)** our time is up for today. **(T)** We can go outside and play on the trampoline **OR** We can go to the kitchen and get a snack" (have options prepared ahead of time that you know your child would look forward to)*

CHILD-PARENT-RELATIONSHIP (C-P-R) TRAINING
Play Session Notes—Session 4

Play Session # ________________ Date: ________________

Significant Happenings:

What I Learned About My Child:

Feelings Expressed:

Play Themes:

What I Learned About Myself:

My feelings during the play session:

What I think I was best at:

What was hardest or most challenging for me:

Questions or Concerns:

Skill I Want to Focus on in the Next Play Session: ________________________________

CHILD-PARENT-RELATIONSHIP (C-P-R) TRAINING
Parent Notes and Homework—Session 5

RULE OF THUMB TO REMEMBER:

1. **"If you can't say it in 10 words or less, don't say it."** As parents, we have a tendency to over-explain to our children, and our message gets lost in the words.
2. **Nothing at this moment is more important than my relationship with my child.** When unsure of what to say to your child or what to do, ask yourself, "What action or words will most preserve the relationship or do least harm?" In moments when no one will win or you will damage the relationship, walking away and saying nothing, or telling your child, "I need to take a time-out to cool off, and then we can talk," is best.

Notes: (use back for additional notes)

____

____

____

____

____

Homework Assignments:

- ☐ Give each of your children a Sandwich Hug and Sandwich Kiss.
- ☐ Read over handouts prior to play session:
  - *Limit Setting: A-C-T Before It's Too Late!*
  - *Play Session Dos & Don'ts*
  - *Play Session Procedures Checklist*
  - *CPRT Cliff Notes* (from Session 4)
- ☐ Conduct play session (same time and place):
  - Complete *Play Session Notes*.
  - Note what you thought you did well, and select one skill you want to work on in your next play session.
  - If you needed to set a limit during your playtime, describe what happened and what you said or did.
- ☐ Additional Assignment:

___ ***I will bring my video next week (if video-recording at clinic: my appt. day/time ____).***

CHILD-PARENT-RELATIONSHIP (C-P-R) TRAINING
Limit Setting: Why Use the Three-Step A-C-T Method? —Session 5

Acknowledge the feeling
Communicate the limit
Target alternatives

Discuss the different messages that are implied in the following typical parent responses to unacceptable behavior:

- It's probably not a good idea to paint the wall.

  Message: I'm really not sure whether it's okay to paint the wall. It might be okay or it might not.

- You can't paint the walls in here.

  Message: ______________________________.

- I can't let you paint the wall.

  Message: ______________________________.

- Maybe you could paint something else other than the wall.

  Message: ______________________________.

- The rule is you can't paint the wall.

  Message: ______________________________.

- The wall is not for painting on.

  Message: ______________________________.

CHILD-PARENT-RELATIONSHIP (C-P-R) TRAINING
Play Session Notes—Session 5

Play Session # ____________Date: ____________________

Significant Happenings:

What I Learned About My Child:

Feelings Expressed:

Play Themes:

What I Learned About Myself:

My feelings during the play session:

What I think I was best at:

What was hardest or most challenging for me:

Questions or Concerns:

Skill I Want to Focus on in the Next Play Session: __________________________________

CHILD-PARENT-RELATIONSHIP (C-P-R) TRAINING

Play Session Skills Checklist

For In-Class Review of Video-Recorded Play Session—Session 5

Play Session # ____________ Date: ________________

(Note: Indicate ✓ in column if skill was used.)

✓	Skill	Notes/Comments
	Set the Stage/Structured Play Session	
	Conveyed "Be-With" Attitudes Full attention/interested Toes followed nose	
	Allowed Child to Lead Avoided giving suggestions Avoided asking questions Returned responsibility to child	
	Followed Child's Lead Physically on child's level Moved closer when child was involved in play Joined in play when invited	
	Reflective Responding Skills:	
	Reflected child's nonverbal play (Tracking)	
	Reflected child's verbalizations (Content)	
	Reflected child's feelings/wants/wishes	
	Voice tone matched child's intensity/affect	
	Responses were brief and interactive	
	Facial expressions matched child's affect	
	Use of Encouragement/Self-Esteem-Building Responses	
	Set Limits, As Needed, Using A-C-T	

CHILD-PARENT-RELATIONSHIP (C-P-R) TRAINING
Parent Notes and Homework—Session 6

RULES OF THUMB TO REMEMBER:

1. **"Grant in fantasy what you can't grant in reality."** In a play session, it is okay to act out feelings and wishes that in reality may require limits. For example, it's okay for the "baby sister" doll to be thrown out a window in playtime.
2. **"Big choices for big kids, little choices for little kids."** Choices given must be commensurate with child's developmental stage.

Notes: (use back for additional notes)

____

____

____

____

____

Homework Assignments:

- ☐ Read *Choice Giving 101: Teaching Responsibility & Decision Making* and *Advanced Choice Giving: Providing Choices as Consequences.*
- ☐ Read *Common Questions Parents Ask* and mark the top two to three issues you have questions about or write in an issue you are challenged by that is not on the worksheet.
- ☐ Practice giving an empowering choice (A) outside of the play session. If the opportunity arises, you may also want to try giving a choice as a consequence (B), but not when your child is dysregulated/out of control.
  - A. Provide choices for the sole purpose of empowering your child (two positive choices for child, where either choice is acceptable to you and either choice is desirable to child).
    What happened ___________________________
    What you said ___________________________
    How child responded ___________________________
  - B. Practice giving choices as a consequence (where choice giving is used to help your child comply with a necessary action; see *Oreo Cookie Method* example in *Advanced Choice Giving* handout).
    What happened ___________________________
    What you said ___________________________
    How child responded ___________________________
- ☐ Read over handouts prior to play session:
  - *Limit Setting: A-C-T Before It's Too Late!* (from Session 4)
  - *Play Session Dos & Don'ts* (from Session 3)
  - *Play Session Procedures Checklist* (from Session 3)
  - *CPRT Cliff Notes* (from Session 4)
- ☐ Conduct play session (same time and place):
  - Complete *Play Session Notes.*
  - Note what you thought you did well, and select one skill you want to work on in your next play session.
  - If you needed to set a limit, describe what happened and what you said or did.
- ☐ Additional Assignment:

____ ***I will bring my video next week (if video-recording at clinic: my appt. day/time ____).***

CHILD-PARENT-RELATIONSHIP (C-P-R) TRAINING

Choice Giving 101: Teaching Responsibility & Decision Making —Session 6

- **Providing children with age-appropriate choices empowers children** by allowing them a measure of control over their circumstances.
  - Children who feel more empowered and "in control" are more capable of regulating their own behavior, a prerequisite for self-control.
  - Choices require that children tap into their inner resources, rather than relying on parents (external resources) to stop their behavior or solve the problem for them.
  - If parents always intervene, the child learns that "Mom or Dad will stop me if I get out of hand" or "Mom or Dad will figure out a solution if I get in a jam."
- **Presenting children with choices provides opportunities for decision making and problem solving.**
  - Through practice with choice making, children learn to accept responsibility for their choices and actions and learn they are competent and capable.
  - Choice giving facilitates the development of the child's conscience; as children are allowed to learn from their mistakes, they learn to weigh decisions based on possible consequences.
- **Providing children with choices reduces power struggles** between parent and child and, importantly, preserves the child-parent relationship.
  - Both parent and child are empowered. Parent is responsible for, or in control of, providing parameters for choices. Children are responsible for, or in control of, their decision (within parent-determined parameters).

Choice-Giving Strategies

- **Provide age-appropriate choices** that are **equally acceptable to the child and to you** (parent). Remember that you must be willing to live with the choice the child makes.
- Don't use choices to try and manipulate the child to do what you want by presenting one choice that you want the child to choose and a second choice that you know the child won't like.
- **Provide little choices to little kids; big choices to big kids.** *Example: A 3-year-old can only handle choosing between two shirts or two food items.* ***"Sasha, do you want to wear your red dress or your pink dress to school?" "Sasha, do you want an apple or orange with your lunch?"***

Choice Giving to Avoid Potential Problem Behavior and Power Struggles

- Choices can be used *to avoid a potential problem*. Similar to the example above, choices given are equally acceptable to parent and child. In this case, choices are planned in advance by the parent to avoid problems that the child has a history of struggling with. In the example above, if Sasha has trouble getting dressed in the morning, provide a choice of what to wear the evening before (to avoid a struggle the next morning); after she has made the choice, take the dress out of the closet, ready for morning.
- Children who are given the responsibility for making a decision are more likely to abide by the decision.
- In selecting choices to prevent problems, it is very important that parents understand the real problem that their child is struggling with and plan ahead to prevent the problem.
  - If your child always comes home hungry and wants something sweet, but you want him to have a healthy snack, plan ahead by having on hand at least two choices of healthy snacks that your child likes. Before he heads for the ice cream, say:

    "Antonio, I bought grapes and cherries for snack; which would you like?"
  - If you know your 9-year-old child tends to head straight for the couch to watch TV after school, plan ahead to brainstorm alternative options for your child to do after school.

    "Ana, I thought of some things we can do this afternoon before dinner. Do you want to go outside and play catch or help bake a cake for dessert tonight?"

Hint: This is another place where "structuring for success" can be applied by eliminating the majority of unacceptable snack items, instead stocking up on healthy snack items and having acceptable activities planned when children arrive home. Structuring your home environment to minimize conflict allows both you and your child to feel more "in control." Remember: **Be a thermostat!**

CHILD-PARENT-RELATIONSHIP (C-P-R) TRAINING

Advanced Choice Giving: Providing Choices as Consequences—Sessions 6-7

Children need parental guidance and discipline. In many instances, parents must make decisions for children—decisions that children are not mature enough to take responsibility for—such as bedtime, other matters of health and safety, and compliance with household policies and rules. However, parents can provide their children with some measure of control in the situation by providing choices. Parents are reminded of the importance of connecting with their child and being sensitive to their emotional state when giving choices or limiting behavior. Remember the Rule of Thumb: "When a child is drowning, don't try to teach her to swim." When children are feeling upset or out of control, they have difficulty hearing choices and consequences. First connect and help calm your child (co-regulate through reflecting child's feelings in soothing voice), then provide choice or wait until a later time.

Oreo® Cookie Method of Choice Giving (from Choices, Cookies, & Kids video by Dr. Garry Landreth)

Example 1: Three-year-old Isabella is clutching a handful of Oreo® cookies, ready to eat them all (it is right before bedtime, and the parent knows it would not be healthy for Isabella to have all the cookies. But Isabella does not know that—she just knows that she wants cookies!): **"Isabella, you can choose to keep one of the cookies to eat and put the rest back, or you can put all of the cookies back—which do you choose?"** Or, if it is permissible to the parent for Isabella to have two cookies: "Isabella, **you can have one cookie or two—which do you choose?"**

Example 2: Six-year-old Oliver does not want to take his medicine and adamantly tells you so! Taking the medicine is not a choice—that is a given. But the parent can provide the child with some choice in the situation by saying, **"Oliver, you can choose to have apple juice or orange juice with your medicine—which do you choose?"**

Example 3: Eight-year-old Omar is tired and cranky and refuses to get in the car to go home from Grandma and Grandpa's house. **"Omar, you can choose to sit in the middle seat by Daddy, or you can choose to sit in the back seat with Selin—which do you choose?"**

Choice Giving to Enforce Household Policies and Rules

Choice giving can be used to enforce household policies/rules. Begin by working on one at a time. In general, provide two choices—one is phrased positively (consequence for complying with policy), and the other choice (consequence for not complying with policy) is stated as a consequence that you believe your child would not prefer (such as giving up favorite TV show). Consequence for noncompliance should be relevant and logical rather than punitive, and it must be **enforceable.**

Example: A household rule has been established that toys in the family room must be picked up off the floor before dinner (children cannot seem to remember without being told repeatedly, and parent is feeling frustrated with constant reminders and power struggles).

"We are about to institute a new and significant policy within the confines of this domicile" (big words get children's attention!). **"When you choose to pick up your toys before dinner, you choose to watch 30 minutes of television after dinner. When you choose not to pick up your toys before dinner, you choose not to watch television after dinner."** *Note: Be sure to let children know when there are 10-15 minutes before dinner, so they have time to pick up their toys.*

Children may be unable to comply the first time you announce this new policy, because you have just informed them. But what is important is that you begin to allow your children to use their internal resources and self-control to <u>remember</u> the new policy without constant reminders. (Remember that the new policy was implemented because you were frustrated and tired of nagging!) So, the second night, parent says, **"Joaquin and Jamal, dinner will be ready in 10 minutes; it is time to pick up your toys."** Parent walks out. When it is time for dinner, parent goes back into room to announce dinner:

a. The toys have not been picked up—<u>say nothing at that moment.</u> After dinner, go back into family room and announce to children, **"Looks like you decided to not watch television tonight."** Even if children get busy picking up the toys, they have already chosen not to watch TV for this night. **"Oh, you're thinking that if you pick your toys up now that you can watch TV, but the policy is that toys have to be put away before dinner."** After children plead for another chance, *follow through on the consequence*, calmly and empathically stating: **"I know that you wish you would have <u>chosen</u> to put your toys away before dinner, so you could <u>choose</u> to watch TV now. Tomorrow night, you can <u>choose</u> to put your toys away before dinner and choose to watch TV."** *Some children will choose not to watch TV for several nights in a row!*
b. The children are busy picking up toys and have put <u>most</u> of them away. Parent says (as she helps with the <u>few</u> remaining toys to demonstrate spirit of cooperation and prevent delay of dinner), **"It's time for dinner—looks like you've chosen to watch TV after dinner tonight."**

Guidelines for Choice giving in Relation to Limit Setting and Consequences

- Enforce consequence **without fail** and **without anger**.
- Consequence is for "today" only—***each day (or play session) should be a chance for a fresh start; a chance to have learned from the previous decision and resulting consequence; a chance to use internal resources to control "self" and make a different decision.***
- **Reflect** child's choice with empathy, but remain firm. Consistency and follow-through are critical!
- Communicate choices in a matter-of-fact voice—power struggles are likely to result if child hears frustration or anger in parent's voice and believes parent is invested in one choice over another. Child must be free to choose consequence for noncompliance.

Caution: *Once your child has reached the stage of "out of control," your child may not be able to hear and process a choice. Take a step back and focus on your child's feelings, reflecting their feelings empathically while limiting unacceptable behavior.*

Remember the oxygen mask analogy: You (parent) must remain calm and relational during choice giving/limit setting in order for child to perceive that they do have a genuine choice in the situation and avoid power struggle. Parent remains calm, neutral, and relational. You want your child to be successful in choosing!

CHILD-PARENT-RELATIONSHIP (C-P-R) TRAINING
Common Questions Parents Ask—Session 6

Q: My child notices that I talk differently in the play sessions and wants me to talk normally. What should I do?

A: Say, "I sound different to you. That's my way of letting you know I heard what you said. Remember, I'm going to that special class to learn how to play with you." (The child may be saying he notices the parent is different; having a surprise reaction to the verbal attention; annoyed by too much reflection of words; or saying he notices the difference in the parent's reflective-type responses. The child may also be saying he doesn't want the parent to change, because that will mean he must then change and adjust to the parent's new way of responding.)

Q: My child asks many questions during the play sessions and resents my not answering them. What should I do?

A: We always begin by reflecting the child's feelings. "You're angry at me." Sometimes a child feels insecure when a parent changes typical ways of responding and is angry because he doesn't know how to react. Your child may feel insecure and be trying to get your attention the way he has done in the past. Your objective is to encourage your child's self-reliance and self-acceptance. "In our special playtime, the answer can be anything you want it to be." For example, your child might ask, "What should I draw?" You want your child to know he's in charge of his drawing during the special playtime, so you respond, "You've decided to draw, and in this special playtime, you can draw whatever you decide." Our objective is to empower the child, to enable the child to discover his own strengths.

Q: My child just plays and has fun. What am I doing wrong?

A: Nothing. Your child is supposed to use the time however she wants. The relationship you are building with your child during the special playtimes is more important than whether or not your child is working on a problem. As your relationship with your child is strengthened, your child's problem will diminish. Your child may be working on issues through her play that you are not aware of. Remember the lesson of the bandage. What you are doing in the playtimes is working, even when you don't see any change. Children can change as a result of what they do in play sessions with parents or play therapists, even though we are not aware of what they are working on. Your job during the special playtimes is to follow your child's lead and be nonjudgmental, understanding, and accepting of your child. Your empathic responses will help your child focus on the issues that are important to her.

Q: I'm bored. What's the value of this?

A: Being bored in a playtime is not an unusual happening because parents have busy schedules, are on the go a lot, and are not used to sitting and interacting quietly for 30 minutes. You can increase your interest level and involvement in your child's play by responding to what you see in your child's face and asking yourself questions such as "What is he feeling?" "What is he trying to say in his play?" "What does he need from me?" or "What is so interesting to him about the toy or the play?" and by making more tracking responses and reflective responses. The most important thing you can do is continue to be patient with the process of the play sessions.

Q: My child doesn't respond to my comments. How do I know I'm on target?

A: Usually when you are on target, your child will let you know. If she doesn't respond to a reflection, you may want to explore other feelings she might be having or convey that you're trying to understand. For example, if you have reflected "You really are angry!" and your child doesn't respond, you might say, "Or maybe it's not anger you're feeling, maybe you're just feeling really strong and powerful." If your child still doesn't respond, you might say, "Maybe that's not it either. I wonder what it could be that you're feeling."

Q: When is it okay for me to ask questions, and when is it not okay?

A: Most of the time, questions can be rephrased as statements, for example, "I wonder if that's ever happened to you" instead of "Has that ever happened to you?" The only type of questions that are okay in play sessions are spoken as "stage whispers," as in "What should I say?"

Q: My child hates the play sessions. Should I discontinue them?

A: Communicating understanding is always important. Say, "You don't want to have the special playtime. You would rather do something else. Let's have the special playtime for 10 minutes, then you can decide if you want to have the rest of the special playtime or do something else." This response helps your child to feel understood and to feel in control. A child in that position in a relationship is much more likely to compromise. In most cases, a child will get started playing and will decide to have the rest of the playtime.

Q: My child wants the playtime to be longer. Should I extend the session?

A: Even though your child is having lots of fun, the time limit is adhered to because this promotes consistency, affords you an opportunity to be firm, and provides your child with an opportunity to bring himself under control and end a very desirable playtime. Use A-C-T limit setting, being sure to acknowledge your child's feelings. For example, you can say, "You're really having fun and would like to play a lot longer, but our special playtime is over for today. We will have another special playtime next Tuesday." If your child persists, you could say, "Joey, I wish we had more time, too, but our 30 minutes are up for today. We'll get to have another playtime next Tuesday."

Q: My child wants to play with the toys at other times during the week. Is that OK?

A: Allowing your child to play with these toys only during the 30-minute playtimes helps to convey the message that this is a special time, a time just for the two of you, a fun time. Setting the toys apart makes the playtime unique and more desirable. Another reason is that this time with your child is an emotional relationship time; the toys become a part of that emotional relationship during which your child expresses and explores emotional messages through the toys because of the kinds of empathic responses you make. This same kind of emotional exploration cannot occur during other playtimes because you are not there to communicate understanding of your child's play. Additionally, being allowed to play with these toys only during the special playtimes helps your child learn to delay his need for gratification. If you are having trouble keeping your child from playing with the special toy kit, try storing it out of sight on the top shelf of your closet. If that doesn't work, lock it in the trunk of your car.

Q: My child wants me to shoot at him during the play session. What should I do?

A: Set the limit. If your child says, "I'm the bad guy, shoot me," say, "I know you want me to shoot you, but you're not for shooting; I can pretend you're the bad guy getting away, and I'll catch you, or you can draw a picture of the bad guy getting shot."

Q: ____

____

____

____

CHILD-PARENT-RELATIONSHIP (C-P-R) TRAINING
Play Session Notes—Session 6

Play Session # ______________ Date: ________________

Significant Happenings:

What I Learned About My Child:

Feelings Expressed:

Play Themes:

What I Learned About Myself:

My feelings during the play session:

What I think I was best at:

What was hardest or most challenging for me:

Questions or Concerns:

Skill I Want to Focus on in the Next Play Session: ______________________________

CHILD-PARENT-RELATIONSHIP (C-P-R) TRAINING

Play Session Skills Checklist

For In-Class Review of Video-Recorded Play Session—Session 6

Play Session # _____________ Date: ___________________

(Note: Indicate ✓ in column if skill was used.)

✓	Skill	Notes/Comments
	Set the Stage/Structured Play Session	
	Conveyed "Be-With" Attitudes Full attention/interested Toes followed nose	
	Allowed Child to Lead Avoided giving suggestions Avoided asking questions Returned responsibility to child	
	Followed Child's Lead Physically on child's level Moved closer when child was involved in play Joined in play when invited	
	Reflective Responding Skills:	
	Reflected child's nonverbal play (Tracking)	
	Reflected child's verbalizations (Content)	
	Reflected child's feelings/wants/wishes	
	Voice tone matched child's intensity/affect	
	Responses were brief and interactive	
	Facial expressions matched child's affect	
	Use of Encouragement/Self-Esteem-Building Responses	
	Set Limits, As Needed, Using A-C-T	

CHILD-PARENT-RELATIONSHIP (C-P-R) TRAINING
Parent Notes and Homework—Session 7

RULE OF THUMB TO REMEMBER:

"Never do for a child that which he can do for himself."

When you do, you rob your child of the joy of discovery and the opportunity to feel competent. You will never know what your child is capable of unless you allow him to try!

Notes: (use back for additional notes)

____

____

____

____

Homework Assignments:

☐ Read *Esteem-Building Responses*—practice giving at least one esteem-building response *during* your play session. Also practice giving one esteem-building response <u>outside</u> of your play session.

What happened outside of play session ______________________

What you said ______________________

How child responded (verbally or nonverbally) ______________________

☐ Write a note to your child of focus, as well as other children in your family, pointing out a positive character quality you genuinely appreciate about your child (see *Positive Character Qualities handout*). Write the following sentence:

"Dear ____________, I was just thinking about you, and what I was thinking is you are so ______________ (thoughtful, responsible, considerate, loving, etc.). I love you, ________________ (Mom, Dad)."

Continue to write a note each week for 3 weeks (mail first note to child, if possible). Be creative in thinking of places you could leave a note for child to find, e.g., put note in lunchbox.

Reminder: Don't expect a response from your child.

These notes are a way to be intentional in letting your child know that they are special, and you *see* them and their positive qualities. You're adding to their self-concept: Your letter of "You are responsible" internalizes with child as "I am responsible."

When you observe your child exhibiting a positive character quality, provide genuine feedback. For example, you observe your child sharing her snack with her sibling. You can respond by stating, "Alexandria, that was thoughtful of you to share your snack with Jeremiah."

☐ Read over handouts prior to play session:

- *Limit Setting: A-C-T Before It's Too Late!* (from Session 4)
- *Play Session Dos & Don'ts* (from Session 3)
- *Play Session Procedures Checklist* (from Session 3)
- *CPRT Cliff Notes* (from Session 4)

☐ Conduct play session (same time and place):

- Complete *Play Session Notes.*
- Note what you thought you did well, *specifically focus on esteem-building responses*, and select one skill you want to work on in your next play session.
- If you needed to set a limit, describe what happened and what you said or did.

☐ Additional Assignment:

____ ***I will bring my video-recording for next week (if video-recording at clinic: my appt. day/time ___).***

CHILD-PARENT-RELATIONSHIP (C-P-R) TRAINING

Esteem-Building Responses: Developing Your Child's Sense of Competence—Session 7

Rule of Thumb: "Never do for a child that which he can do for himself."

When you do, you rob your child of the joy of discovery and the opportunity to feel competent. You will never know what your child is capable of unless you allow him to try!

Parents help their child develop a positive view of "self," not only by providing their child with love and unconditional acceptance, but also by helping their child feel competent and capable. Parents help their child feel competent and capable by first allowing the child to **experience** what it is like to discover, figure out, and problem-solve. Parents show faith in their child and their child's capabilities by allowing him to struggle with a problem, all the while providing encouragement (encouragement vs. praise is covered in detail in Session 8). For most parents, allowing children to struggle is hard—but it is a necessary process for children to truly feel capable. The next step in helping children develop a positive view of self as competent and capable is learning to respond in ways that give children credit for ideas, effort, and accomplishments, without praising.

Esteem-Building Responses to Use in Play Sessions:

"You did it!"	"You decided that was the way that was supposed to fit together."
"You figured it out."	"You know just how you want that to look."
"You like the way that turned out."	"You're not giving up—you're determined to figure that out."
"You decided. . . "	"You've got a plan for how. . . "

Example 1: Child works and works to get the lid off the Play-Doh and finally gets it off.
Parent response: **"You did it!"** (affect in your voice matches child's affect; don't be over-enthusiastic)

Example 2: Child works and works to get the lid off the Play-Doh but can't get it off.
Parent response: **"You're determined to figure that out."**

Example 3: Child struggles to get the dart to fit into the gun and pushed in all the way and finally gets it in.
Parent response: **"You figured it out."**

Example 4: Child spends time drawing, cutting, and gluing a nondescript piece of "art" and shows you with a smile when he is finished.
Parent response: **"You really like the way that turned out."**

Example 5: Child is carefully setting up army soldiers and telling you all about a battle that is going to take place, what is going to happen, and how one side is going to sneak up, and so forth.
Parent response: **"You've got a plan for how that side is going to. . ."** or **"You've got that all planned out."**

Note: If your child tends to ask you to do things for him without trying first, ask the therapist to role-play how to return responsibility to your child to do things he is capable of figuring out for himself.

****

The Struggle to Become a Butterfly: A True Story (Author Unknown)

A family in my neighborhood once brought in two cocoons that were just about to hatch. They watched as the first one began to open and the butterfly inside squeezed very slowly and painfully through a tiny hole that it chewed in one end of the cocoon. After lying exhausted for about 10 minutes following its agonizing emergence, the butterfly finally flew out the open window on its beautiful wings.

The family decided to help the second butterfly so that it would not have to go through such an excruciating ordeal. So, as it began to emerge, they carefully sliced open the cocoon with a razor blade, doing the equivalent of a Caesarean section. The second butterfly never did sprout wings, and in about 10 minutes, instead of flying away, it quietly died.

The family asked a biologist friend to explain what had happened. The scientist said that the difficult struggle to emerge from the small hole actually pushes liquids from deep inside the butterfly's body cavity into the tiny capillaries in the wings, where they harden to complete the healthy and beautiful adult butterfly.

Remember: WITHOUT THE STRUGGLE, THERE ARE NO WINGS!

CHILD-PARENT-RELATIONSHIP (C-P-R) TRAINING
Positive Character Qualities—Session 7

Affectionate	brave	calm	careful
Caring	clever	compassionate	confident
Considerate	cooperative	courageous	creative
Dependable	determined	empathic	energetic
Enthusiastic	friendly	fun	generous
Gentle	good sport	helpful	honest
Humble	insightful	joyful	kind
Loving	loyal	modest	neat
Patient	persistent	polite	punctual
Reliable	resourceful	respectful	responsible
Sensitive	sincere	smart	supportive
team player	thoughtful	trustworthy	unique

Note: the above table of character qualities was contributed by Sandra Blackard, M.A.

CHILD-PARENT-RELATIONSHIP (C-P-R) TRAINING
Play Session Notes—Session 7

Play Session # ____________ Date: ____________

Significant Happenings:

What I Learned About My Child:

Feelings Expressed:

Play Themes:

What I Learned About Myself:

My feelings during the play session:

What I think I was best at:

What was hardest or most challenging for me:

Questions or Concerns:

Skill I Want to Focus on in the Next Play Session: ______________________________

CHILD-PARENT-RELATIONSHIP (C-P-R) TRAINING
Play Session Skills Checklist
For In-Class Review of Video-Recorded Play Session—Session 7

Play Session ____________________ Date: ____________________

(Note: Indicate ✓ in column if skill was used.)

✓	Skill	Notes/Comments
	Set the Stage/Structured Play Session	
	Conveyed "Be-With" Attitudes Full attention/interested Toes followed nose	
	Allowed Child to Lead Avoided giving suggestions Avoided asking questions Returned responsibility to child	
	Followed Child's Lead Physically on child's level Moved closer when child was involved in play Joined in play when invited	
	Reflective Responding Skills:	
	Reflected child's nonverbal play (Tracking)	
	Reflected child's verbalizations (Content)	
	Reflected child's feelings/wants/wishes	
	Voice tone matched child's intensity/affect	
	Responses were brief and interactive	
	Facial expressions matched child's affect	
	Use of Encouragement/Self-Esteem-Building Responses	
	Set Limits, As Needed, Using A-C-T	

CHILD-PARENT-RELATIONSHIP (C-P-R) TRAINING
Parent Notes and Homework—Session 8

RULE OF THUMB TO REMEMBER:

"Encourage the effort rather than praise the product!"

Children need encouragement like a plant needs water.

Notes: (use back for additional notes)

____

____

____

____

____

____

Homework Assignments:

☐ Read *Encouragement vs. Praise*—practice giving at least one encouragement response *during* your play session. Also practice giving at least one encouragement outside of your play session.

What happened or what child said (outside of play session) ______________________________

What you said ______________________________

How child responded (verbally or nonverbally) ______________________________

☐ Write down one issue you are struggling with outside of play session time that you would like help with.

____

☐ Read over handouts prior to play session:

- *Limit Setting: A-C-T Before It's Too Late!* (from Session 4)
- *Play Session Dos & Don'ts* (from Session 3)
- *Play Session Procedures Checklist* (from Session 3)
- *CPRT Cliff Notes* (from Session 4)

☐ Conduct play session (same time and place):

- Complete *Play Session Notes*.
- Note what you thought you did well, *specifically focus on encouragement responses*, and select one skill you want to work on in your next play session.
- Note use of encouraging responses used.

☐ Additional Assignment:

Write second note to your child of focus, as well as other children in the family, pointing out another positive character quality you appreciate about the child. (Vary how the note is delivered, for example, place it in the child's lunchbox, tape it to the mirror in the bathroom, place it on the child's pillow or under the child's dinner plate, etc.)

____ ***I will bring my video next week (if video-recording at clinic: my appt. day/time____).***

CHILD-PARENT-RELATIONSHIP (C-P-R) TRAINING
Encouragement vs. Praise—Session 8

Rule of Thumb: "Encourage the effort rather than praise the product."

Praise: Although praise and encouragement both focus on positive behaviors and appear to be the same process, praise actually fosters dependence in children by teaching them to rely on an external source of control and motivation rather than on self-control and self-motivation.

- Praise is an attempt to motivate children with external rewards. In effect, the parent who praises is saying, "If you do something I consider good, you will have the reward of being recognized and valued by me."
- Overreliance on praise can produce crippling effects. Children come to believe that their worth depends upon the opinions of others. Praise employs words that place value judgments on children and focuses on external evaluation.

Examples of Praise: "You're such a good boy/girl." Your child may wonder, "*Am I accepted only when I'm good?*"
"You got an A. That's great!" Your child may wonder, "*Am I worthwhile only when I make As?*"
"You did a good job." "I'm so proud of you." The message sent is that your (parent's) evaluation is more important than your child's.

Encouragement: Focuses on internal evaluation and the contributions children make—facilitates development of self-motivation and self-control. Encouraging parents teach their children to accept their own inadequacies, learn from mistakes (mistakes are wonderful opportunities for learning), have confidence in themselves, and feel useful through contribution.

- When commenting on children's efforts, be careful not to place value judgments on what they have done. Be alert to eliminate value-laden words (good, great, excellent, etc.) from your vocabulary at these times. Instead, substitute words of encouragement that help children believe in themselves.
- Encouragement <u>focuses on effort</u> and <u>can always be given</u>. Children who feel their efforts are encouraged, valued, and appreciated develop qualities of persistence and determination and tend to be good problem-solvers.

Note: Parent's voice should match child's level of affect; if child is excited about getting an "A" on a test, parent responds likewise with excitement in her voice, "You're really proud of that!" Use after-the-event celebrations (based on child's pride in achievement) instead of rewards (external motivators to get the child to achieve) to recognize achievement. In the above example, the parent could add, "Sounds like something to celebrate; let's make a cake!" or "You choose the restaurant, my treat!"

<u>**Encouraging Phrases That Recognize Effort and Improvement:**</u>

"You did it!" or "You got it!"
"You really worked hard on that."
"You didn't give up until you figured it out."
"Look at the progress you've made. . . " (Be specific.)
"You answer the questions about sports really fast!"

<u>**Encouraging Phrases That Show Confidence:**</u>

"That's a rough one, but I bet you'll figure it out."
"I have confidence in you. You'll figure it out."
"Sounds like you have a plan."
"Sounds like you know a lot about ____________________________."

<u>**Encouraging Phrases That Focus on Contributions, Assets, and Appreciation:**</u>

"Thanks, that was a big help."
"It was thoughtful of you to ___________" or "I appreciate that you ___________."
"You have a knack for __________. Can you give me a hand with that?"
"It took a lot of courage to do that and you did it."

<u>**In Summary, Encouragement Is:**</u>

1. Valuing and accepting children as they are (not putting conditions on acceptance).
2. Pointing out the positive aspects of behavior.
3. Showing faith in children, so that they can come to believe in themselves.
4. Recognizing effort and improvement (rather than requiring achievement).
5. Showing appreciation for contributions.

Adapted from Dinkmeyer, D., & McKay, G. D. (1982). <u>The Parent's Handbook</u>. Circle Pines, MN: American Guidance Service.

CHILD-PARENT-RELATIONSHIP (C-P-R) TRAINING
Play Session Notes—Session 8

Play Session ________________ Date: __________________

Significant Happenings:

What I Learned About My Child:

Feelings Expressed:

Play Themes:

What I Learned About Myself:

My feelings during the play session:

What I think I was best at:

What was hardest or most challenging for me:

Questions or Concerns:

Skill I Want to Focus on in the Next Play Session: ________________________________

CHILD-PARENT-RELATIONSHIP (C-P-R) TRAINING
Play Session Skills Checklist
For In-Class Review of Video-Recorded Play Session—Session 8

Play Session ________________ Date: ________________

(Note: Indicate ✓ in column if skill was used.)

✓	Skill	Notes/Comments
	Set the Stage/Structured Play Session	
	Conveyed "Be-With" Attitudes Full attention/interested Toes followed nose	
	Allowed Child to Lead Avoided giving suggestions Avoided asking questions Returned responsibility to child	
	Followed Child's Lead Physically on child's level Moved closer when child was involved in play Joined in play when invited	
	Reflective Responding Skills:	
	Reflected child's nonverbal play (Tracking)	
	Reflected child's verbalizations (Content)	
	Reflected child's feelings/wants/wishes	
	Voice tone matched child's intensity/affect	
	Responses were brief and interactive	
	Facial expressions matched child's affect	
	Use of Encouragement/Self-Esteem-Building Responses	
	Set Limits, As Needed, Using A-C-T	

CHILD-PARENT-RELATIONSHIP (C-P-R) TRAINING
Parent Notes and Homework—Session 9

RULES OF THUMB TO REMEMBER:

1. **"Where there are no limits, there is no security."** Consistent Limits = Security in the Relationship. When you don't follow through, you lose credibility and harm your relationship with your child.
2. **"Don't try to change everything at once!"** Focus on "big" issues that ultimately will mean the most to your child's development of positive self-esteem and feelings of competence.

Notes: (use back for additional notes)

____

____

Homework Assignments:

- ☐ Review *Advanced Limit Setting* and Generalizing Limit Setting to Outside the Play Session. Think of a limit setting situation that you anticipate that your child might have difficulty complying with during a play session (or in the past has not complied) and describe on *Advanced Limit Setting* handout and note how you might respond.
- ☐ Describe a time you used A-C-T outside of the play session this week.
  - What happened ____
  - What you said ____
  - How child responded (verbally or nonverbally) ____________________
- ☐ Notice the number of times you touch your child in interactions outside the play session (hugging, patting on the head, a touch on the arm, etc.) and keep count this week. # of physical contacts: ________
- ☐ A related assignment is to play-wrestle with your children. (Example: In a two-parent family with small children, Mom and kids can sneak up on Dad and try to get him down on the floor, accompanied by lots of fun and laughter.)
- ☐ Report on use of C-P-R responses used outside of play session this week. What went well and what didn't? ____

  ____
- ☐ Read over handouts prior to play session:
  - *Limit Setting: A-C-T Before It's Too Late!* (from Session 4)
  - *Play Session Dos & Don'ts* (from Session 3)
  - *Play Session Procedures Checklist* (from Session 3)
  - CPRT Cliff Notes (from Session 4)
- ☐ Conduct play session (same time and place):
  - Complete *Play Session Notes.*
  - Note what you thought you did well, and select one skill you want to work on in your next play session.
  - Note any limits setting situations and how you responded.
- ☐ Additional Assignment:
  Write third note to your child of focus, as well as other children in the family, pointing out <u>another</u> positive character quality you appreciate about the child. (Vary how the note is delivered.)

_____ ***I will bring my video next week (if video-recording at clinic: my appt. day/time ______).***

CHILD-PARENT-RELATIONSHIP (C-P-R) TRAINING

Advanced Limit Setting: Giving Choices as Consequences for Noncompliance—Session 9

Play Session Example: After parent has stated that the Play-Doh is for playing with on the tray, 5-year-old Damian dumps it on the floor.

Step 1. Parent follows the A-C-T method of limit setting: "**Damian, I know that you want to play with the Play-Doh over there, but the floor (carpet, etc.) is not for putting Play-Doh on; (pointing to tray) the tray is for putting the Play-Doh on.**" Damian continues to ignore parent and begins to smash the Play-Doh on the floor.

Step 2. Parent may patiently restate limit up to three times before beginning Step 3.

Note: This example (restating limit up to three times) assumes that parent has chosen a location for the play session where the floor surface can be easily cleaned by parent after special playtime.

Step 3. "If-Then" choices (consequences) for following or not following limit.

Begin "**If-Then**" choice-giving method to provide consequence for unacceptable behavior. Note the number of times the words "choose" or "choice" are used! Remember that the intent is for the child to bring himself under control; therefore, patience is the order of the day. Children need time and practice to learn self-control.

Example: "**Damian, If you choose to play with the Play-Doh on the tray (pointing to tray), then you choose to play with the Play-Doh today. If you choose to continue to play with the Play-Doh on the floor, then you choose not to play with the Play-Doh for the rest of today.**" (Pause.)

- Patiently restate if child does not make the choice to comply with the limit. (If Damian doesn't answer and continues to play with Play-Doh on floor, then he has made his choice.) "**Damian, it looks like you've chosen to put the Play-Doh up for today. You can choose to give me the Play-Doh, or you can choose for me to put the Play-Doh up for you; which do you choose?**"
- If child begins to cry and beg for the Play-Doh, parent must be tough and follow through, acknowledging child's feelings and giving child hope that he will have a chance to make a different choice in the next play session. "**Damian, I understand that you're unhappy that you chose to have the Play-Doh put up for today, but you can choose to play with it in our next playtime.**"

In the above example, if at any point the child took the Play-Doh and put it on the tray to play with, the parent must be careful to respond matter-of-factly, "**Looks like you decided you wanted to play with it some more today.**"

Practice:

1. Your child aims a loaded dart gun at you.

A **[Child's name],** ______________________________,

C *but* ______________________________.

T *You can* ______________________________.

Your child continues to aim the gun at you after you have set the limit using A-C-T three times.

[Child's name], if you choose to *aim the gun at me,*
then you choose *not to play with the gun today.*

If your child continues to aim the gun at you (whether he shoots the gun or not), you say:
[Child's name], looks like you've chosen not to play with the gun for the rest of today.

If your child shoots the gun at the bop bag or another acceptable place, you say (matter-of-factly):
Looks like you decided to play with the gun some more today.

2. Describe a situation in which you think you might need to set a limit during the play session and you anticipate the child might not comply.

   Situation: ____

   ____

   ____

   ____

   A ____

   C ____

   T ____

   If/Then ____

   ____

   ____

   ____

   ____

   ____

CHILD-PARENT-RELATIONSHIP (C-P-R) TRAINING
Generalizing Limit Setting to Outside the Play Session—Session 9

Acknowledge the feeling

Communicate the limit

Target alternatives

Example #1

Your 6-year-old child, Olivia, wants a My Little Pony stuffed toy from the "claw" game at the movie theater. The rest of your family is walking into the theater and Olivia is standing cross-armed, insisting on playing the game.

1. Acknowledge your child's feelings (*your voice must convey genuine empathy and understanding*).
   "Olivia, I know you *really* want to play that." *(She learns her feelings and desires are valid and acceptable.)*

2. Communicate the limit (be specific, clear, and brief).
   "But, it's not game time; It's movie time!" *(This response may be enough to help Olivia bring self under control and go into the movie with you).*

3. Target acceptable alternatives. (Provide one or more choices, depending on age of child.)
   "You can choose to walk with me into the movie or you can choose to walk with Daddy and Joey into the movie." (If you are not okay with her playing the game at all.)

   Or

   "You can choose to play that after the movie." (If you are okay with her playing the game.)

The goal of targeting alternatives is to provide your child with acceptable alternatives—ones that are acceptable to your child and you (parent), and ones that you believe will help child get their needs met. In the above example, Olivia wanted to do something fun and also maybe wanted to decide how things went that day. With the alternatives presented, Olivia's need for fun and decision-making power were both met (movie and choice).

TIP! Simply recognizing and acknowledging your child's feelings and desires can often defuse the intensity of the feeling or need.

- Oftentimes, children have emotional needs underneath the surface of the situation. Olivia may have been feeling left out that day. So, her insistence about playing the game may be less about the prize and more about wanting to be attended to relationally. Acknowledging her feelings and presenting alternatives to *Be-With* others would help meet this underlying need for relationship.
- Patiently restate the limit up to three times, depending on the age of the child, to allow child to struggle with self-control before proceeding to the next step.

4. Choice giving (consequences) as next step after noncompliance. Example: Olivia continues to refuse to walk into the movie and insists on playing the game now.
   "Olivia, playing this game now is not one of the choices. <u>You can choose</u> to see the movie and <u>choose</u> to play the game afterwards, or <u>you can choose</u> to stay here with me and <u>choose</u> not to play the game afterwards."
   If child starts walking away, even slowly, parent may state: **"That was a hard decision for you. Looks like you are choosing to watch the movie now and play the game later."**

If child does not choose, parent may state: **"If you choose to not choose, you choose for me to choose for you."**

If child continues to insist on playing the game now, parent can state: **"I see you've chosen to stay out here with me and to not play the game later."**

TIP! When child pushes limits, parent increases empathy! Before the situation escalates into choices as consequences, be sure to give child ample time to relax and make a choice.

Remember the **Rule of Thumb: "When a child is drowning, don't try to teach them to swim."** In this moment of stress, Olivia is in fight-flight-or-freeze mode, neurobiologically, and therefore needs you to **CONNECT** with her and acknowledge her feelings and be patient in order for her to relax enough to be able to engage her prefrontal cortex to make a choice. After all, your goal is not to "win"—the goal of limit setting is for you (parent) to provide your child with consistent opportunity to develop internal coping strategies and decision-making skills.

- In this example, even the last choice of spending time with her parent and not playing the game presents Olivia with the opportunity for quality time with her parent. If after Olivia relaxes in the lobby, she says, "*Mommy, can we go watch the movie now and play the game after?*" you respond empathetically ***"Remember when you chose to stay here with me instead of going into the movie—at that very moment, you chose to not play the game today, but we can go watch the movie now."*** Your child may continue to plead and cry (because it has worked in the past). BE FIRM—don't give in! Your child's *choices* matter.

What To Do After A-C-T

After you've followed the three-step A-C-T process with empathy and firmness:

1. If you are satisfied with your response to the child's question and the question or plea is repeated, DON'T DISCUSS FURTHER.
2. If you think the child doesn't understand your response, say:

   — "I've already answered that question. You must have some question about my answer."
3. If you think the child understands, say:

   — "I can tell you'd like to discuss this some more, but I've already answered that question."

   OR

   — "I can tell you don't like my answer. If you are asking again because you want me to change my mind, I will not."

   OR

   — "Do you remember the answer I gave you a few minutes ago when you asked that same question?" If child answers, "No, I don't remember," say, "Go sit down in a quiet place and think. I know you'll be able to remember."
4. If you are not satisfied with your response to your child's question:

   — If you are open to persuasion, say:

   "I don't know. Let's sit down and discuss it."

   — If you intend to answer the question later but are not prepared to answer now, say:

   "I can't answer that question now because (I want to talk it over with someone; I want to get more infor-mation; I want to think about it, etc.). I'll let you know (specific time)."

   — If child demands an answer now, say:

   "If you must have an answer now, the answer will have to be 'NO."

What To DO When Limit Setting Doesn't Work

You have been careful <u>several times</u> to calmly and empathically use **A-C-T and Choice-Giving**. Your child continues to deliberately disobey. What do you do?

- ☐ <u>Look for natural causes for rebellion</u>: Fatigue, sickness, hunger, stress, and so forth. Take care of physical needs and crises before expecting cooperation.
- ☐ <u>Remain in control, respecting yourself and your child</u>: You are not a failure if your child rebels, and your child is not bad. All kids need to "practice" rebelling. Remember: At this very moment, nothing is more important than your relationship with your child, so respond in a way that respects your child and yourself. *If you find yourself feeling angry at your child and losing control, walk outside or to another room.*
- ☐ <u>Remember the Brain</u>: Sometimes children can become so dysregulated that they are not capable in the moment of making a choice. The hand model of the brain by Dr. Dan Siegel is an excellent reminder of how to understand and support young children during these times. Can access at this link: https://www.youtube.com/watch?v=gm9CIJ74Oxw
- ☐ <u>Set reasonable consequences for disobedience</u>: Let your child choose to obey or disobey, but set a reason¬able consequence for disobedience. Example: "If you choose to watch TV instead of going to bed, then you choose to give up TV all day tomorrow" (or whatever is a meaningful consequence for child).
- ☐ <u>Never tolerate violence</u>: Physically restrain your child who becomes violent, without becoming aggressive yourself. Empathically and calmly **REFLECT** your child's anger and loneliness; provide compassionate control and alternatives as child begins to regain control.
- ☐ <u>If your child refuses to choose, you choose for them</u>: Your child's refusal to choose is also a choice. Set the con¬sequences. Example: "If you choose not to (choice A or B), then you have chosen for me to choose for you."
- ☐ <u>ENFORCE THE CONSEQUENCES</u>: Don't state consequences that you cannot enforce. If you crumble under your child's anger or tears, you have abdicated your role as parent and lost your power. **GET TOUGH!** When you <u>don't follow through</u>, you lose credibility and harm your relationship with your child.
- ☐ <u>Recognize signs of more serious problems</u>: Depression, trauma (abuse/neglect/extreme grief/stress). The chronically angry or rebellious child is in emotional trouble and may need professional help. Share your con¬cern with your child. Example: "John, I've noticed that you seem to be angry and unhappy most of the time. I love you, and I'm worried about you. We're going to get help so we can all be happier."

CHILD-PARENT-RELATIONSHIP (C-P-R) TRAINING

Play Session Notes—Session 9

Play Session # _______________ Date: _______________

Significant Happenings:

What I Learned About My Child:

Feelings Expressed:

Play Themes:

What I Learned About Myself:

My feelings during the play session:

What I think I was best at:

What was hardest or most challenging for me:

Questions or Concerns:

Skill I Want to Focus on in the Next Play Session: _______________________________

CHILD-PARENT-RELATIONSHIP (C-P-R) TRAINING

Play Session Skills Checklist

For In-Class Review of Video-Recorded Play Session—Session 9

Play Session # ______________ Date: ______________

(Note: Indicate ✓ in column if skill was used.)

✓	Skill	Notes/Comments
	Set the Stage/Structured Play Session	
	Conveyed "Be-With" Attitudes Full attention/interested Toes followed nose	
	Allowed Child to Lead Avoided giving suggestions Avoided asking questions Returned responsibility to child	
	Followed Child's Lead Physically on child's level Moved closer when child was involved in play Joined in play when invited	
	Reflective Responding Skills:	
	Reflected child's nonverbal play (Tracking)	
	Reflected child's verbalizations (Content)	
	Reflected child's feelings/wants/wishes	
	Voice tone matched child's intensity/affect	
	Responses were brief and interactive	
	Facial expressions matched child's affect	
	Use of Encouragement/Self-Esteem-Building Responses	
	Set Limits, As Needed, Using A-C-T	

CHILD-PARENT-RELATIONSHIP (C-P-R) TRAINING
Parent Notes and Homework—Session 10

☝ RULES OF THUMB TO REMEMBER:

"Good things come in small packages."

Don't wait for big events to enter into your child's world the little ways are always with us. Hold onto precious moments!

Always remember: "Nothing at this moment is more important than my relationship with my child."

Notes: (use back for additional notes)

____

____

____

____

____

Homework Assignments:

- ☐ Continue play sessions: If you stop now, the message is that you were playing with your child because you had to, not because you wanted to:

  I agree to continue my play sessions with my child of focus for ___ weeks and/or begin sessions with ____________________ and do for ___ weeks.
- ☐ Date and time for follow-up meetings: __________________________
- ☐ Volunteer meeting coordinator: __________________________

Recommended Reading:

For Parents

- *Relational Parenting* (2000) and *How to Really Love Your Child* (1992), Ross Campbell
- *Between Parent and Child* (1956), Haim Ginott
- *Liberated Parents, Liberated Children* (1990), Adele Faber and Elaine Mazlish
- *How to Talk So Kids Will Listen and Listen So Kids Will Talk* (2012), Adele Faber and Elaine Mazlish
- *"SAY WHAT YOU SEE" for Parents and Teachers* (2005), Sandra Blackard (free online resource available at www.languageoflistening.com)
- *The Parent Survival Guide* (2009), Theresa Kellam
- *The Whole-Brain Child: 12 Revolutionary Strategies to Nurture Your Child's Developing Mind* (2011), Daniel Siegel and Tina Payne Bryson

- *No Drama Discipline: The Whole-Brain Way to Calm the Chaos and Nurture Your Child's Developing Mind* (2014), Daniel Siegel and Tina Payne Bryson
- *Parenting from the Inside Out* (2014), Daniel Siegel and Mary Hartzell
- *Brain Based Parenting* (2012), Daniel Hughes and Jonathan Baylin
- *Positive Discipline* (2006), Jane Nelson

For Children

- *No Matter What*, Debi Gliori
- *Love You Forever*, Robert Munsch
- *A Mother's Wish*, Kathy-Jo Wargin
- *The Dot*, Peter Reynolds
- *What Do You Do with an Idea?* Kobi Yamada
- *Not a Box*, Antoinette Portis
- *I Wish You More*, Amy Krouse Rosenthal
- *The Kissing Hand*, Audrey Penn
- *Guess How Much I Love You*, Sam McBratney
- *The Invisible String*, Patrice Karst
- *My Many-Colored Days*, Dr. Seuss
- *Alexander and the Terrible, Horrible, No Good, Very Bad Day*, Judith Viorst

CHILD-PARENT-RELATIONSHIP (C-P-R) TRAINING
Rules of Thumb and Other Things to Remember—Session 10

Rules of Thumb

1. **Focus on the donut, not the hole!**
   Focus on the relationship (your strengths and your child's strengths), NOT the problem.
2. **Be a thermostat, not a thermometer!**
   Learn to RESPOND (reflect) rather than REACT. Your child's feelings are not your feelings. Your feelings and behavior need not escalate with your child's.
3. **What's most important may not be what you do, but what you do after what you have done!**
   We are certain to make mistakes, but we can recover. It is how we handle our mistakes that makes the difference.
4. **Your toes should follow your nose.**
   Body language conveys interest.
5. **You can't give away what you do not possess.**
   (Analogy: oxygen mask on airplane) You can't extend patience and acceptance to your child if you can't first offer it to yourself.
6. **When a child is drowning, don't try to teach her to swim.**
   When a child is feeling upset or out of control, that is not the moment to impart a rule or teach a lesson.
7. **During play sessions, limits are not needed until they are needed!**
8. **If you can't say it in 10 words or less, don't say it.**
   As parents, we tend to over-explain, and our message gets lost in the words.
9. **Grant in fantasy what you can't grant in reality.**
   In a play session, it is okay to act out feelings and wishes that in reality may require limits.
10. **Big choices for big kids, little choices for little kids.**
    Choices given must be commensurate with child's developmental stage.
11. **Never do for a child that which he can do for himself.**
    You will never know what your child is capable of unless you allow him to try!
12. **Encourage the effort rather than praise the product.**
    Children need encouragement like a plant needs water.
13. **Don't try to change everything at once!**
    Focus on "big" issues that ultimately will mean the most to your child's development of positive self-esteem and feelings of competence.
14. **Where there are no limits, there is no security.** (Consistent Limits = Secure Relationship)
    When you don't follow through, you lose credibility and harm your relationship with your child.
15. **Good things come in small packages.**
    Don't wait for big events to enter into your child's world—the little ways are always with us. Hold on to precious moments!

CHILD-PARENT-RELATIONSHIP (C-P-R) TRAINING
Page 2—Rules of Thumb and Other Things to Remember—Session 10

Other Things to Remember

1. Reflective responses help children to feel understood and can lessen anger.
2. In play, children express what their lives are like now, what their needs are, or how they wish things could be. Children with a history of traumatic experiences may play out past events as they experience them in the present.
3. In the playtimes, the parent is not the source of answers (reflect questions back to the child: "Hmm—I wonder").
4. Don't ask questions you already know the answer to.
5. Questions imply non-understanding. Questions put children in their minds. Children live in their hearts.
6. What's important is not what the child knows, but what the child believes.
7. When you focus on the problem, you lose sight of the child.
8. Support the child's feeling, intent, or need, even if you can't support the child's behavior.
9. Noticing the child is a powerful builder of self-esteem.
10. Empower children by giving them credit for making decisions: "You decided to ________."
11. One of the best things we can communicate to our children is that they are competent. Tell children they are capable, and they will think they are capable. If you tell children enough times they can't do something, sure enough, they can't.
12. Encourage creativity and freedom—with freedom comes responsibility.
13. "We're about to institute a new and significant policy immediately effective within the confines of this domicile."
14. When we are flexible in our approach, we can handle anger much more easily (when parents are rigid in their approach, both parent and child can end up hurt).
15. When unsure of what to say to child or what to do, ask yourself, "What action or words will most preserve the relationship or do least harm?" Sometimes walking away and saying nothing, or telling the child, "I need to take a time-out to cool off, and then we can talk," is best. Always remember: "Nothing at this moment is more important than my relationship with my child." (Also applies to spouses, significant others, etc.)
16. Live in the moment—today is enough. Don't push children toward the future.

CPRT TRAINING RESOURCES

Using CPRT Training Resources

The *CPRT Training Resources* include a list of resources for professionals and parents organized by videos, books, and manuals. Each of these categories is further divided into recommended and supplemental resources.

Note: Additional resources specific to the population of interest are included in the four new protocols on the Companion Website.

VIDEOS

Recommended Videos

Center for Play Therapy (Producer), & Landreth, G. (Writer/Director). (1994). *Choices, cookies, & kids: A creative approach to discipline* [Video cassette-DVD]. Approximate length: 35 minutes. (Available in VHS and DVD from Center for Play Therapy, www.centerforplaytherapy.com, University of North Texas, P.O. Box 310829, Denton, TX 76203-1337, 940-565-3864).

Child Parent Relationship Therapy (CPRT) in action: Four couples in a CPRT group (2013) with Drs. S. C. Bratton & G. Landreth. Available at www.centerforplaytherapy.com. Video demonstrates the process and delivery of content of CPRT to view prior to conducting CPRT. Two DVDs, 4 hours of training.

Child Parent Relationship Therapy (CPRT) parent-child play session skills demonstration video (in press). Bratton, S. & Landreth, G. (Producers and Writer/Directors). Video is useful to demonstrate CPRT play session skills to parents.

Nova Presentation (Producer). *Life's first feelings* [Video cassette]. Available on www.amazon.com, Item No. 4810. *The following two segments are used in CPRT Training Session 1 to help parents understand the importance of responding appropriately to children's feelings. Prior to showing to parents, filial therapists should view entire video for helpful, research-based information on the universality of the development of emotions, as well as information on child temperament and child's innate internal locus of control. (Can also be found on YouTube, however time markers would below will not apply)*

Segment Info: 0:00 Video Begins (*times listed are "real time," not "counter time"*)
5:14 Segment 1 Begins: Parent Responsive/Non-Responsive to Infant
9:46 Segment 1 Ends (*Total time = 4min. 32 sec*)
21:34 Segment 2 Begins: Universal Feelings/Facial Expressions
27:01 Segment 2 Ends (*Total time = 5min. 27 sec*)

Supplemental Videos

Center for Play Therapy (Producer), & Landreth, G. (Writer/Director). (1997). *Child-centered play therapy: A clinical session* [Video cassette-DVD]. (Available from Center for Play Therapy, www.centerforplaytherapy.com, University of North Texas, P.O. Box 310829, Denton, TX 76203-1337, 940-565-3864). (1) This video is useful for demonstration of play session skills for filial therapist that do not have their own video sessions (with permission to show parents). (2) This video contains several "segments" that can be utilized to teach specific filial play skills. *The following 5-minute segment is particularly helpful in demonstrating "Being With" and allowing the child to lead as well as basic play session skills.*

Segment Info: 0:00 Video Begins
42:11 Medical play segment begins
47:12 Medical play segment ends

National Institute of Relationships Enhancement (Producer), & Guerney, L. (Writer/Director). (1989). *Filial therapy with Louise Guerney* [Video cassette]. (Available from 12500 Blake Road Silver Spring, MD 20904-2050). *Contains examples of parent-child play sessions*).

VanFleet, R. (Writer/Director). (1999). *Introduction to filial play therapy* (Available from Family Enhancement & Play Therapy Center, P.O. Box 613, Boiling Springs, PA 17007).

BOOKS AND MANUALS

Required Resources

Bratton, S., & Landreth, G. (2020). *Child Parent Relationship Therapy (CPRT) treatment manual: An evidence-based 10-session filial therapy model* (2nd ed.). New York, NY: Routledge. *The manual is accompanied by a Companion Website (www.routledge.com/cw/bratton) that includes all training materials for ease of reproduction.*

Landreth, G., & Bratton, S. (2020). *Child Parent Relationship Therapy (CPRT): An evidence-based 10-session filial therapy model* (2nd ed.). New York, NY: Routledge.

Supplemental Therapist Resources

Bailey, B. (2000). *I love you rituals.* New York, NY: HarperCollins.

Campbell, R. (1992). *How to really love your child.* Colorado Springs, CO: Chariot Victor.

Campbell, R. (2000). *Relational parenting.* Chicago, IL: Moody Press.

Faber, A., & Mazlish, E. (1990). *Liberated parents/Liberated children.* New York, NY: Avon Books.

Faber, A., & Mazlish, E. (2002). *How to talk so kids will listen & listen so kids will talk.* New York, NY: Harper Collins.

Ginott, H. (2003). *Between parent and child* revised edition. New York, NY: Avon Books.

Guerney, L. (1987). *The parenting skills program: Leader's manual.* State College, PA: IDEALS.

Guerney, L. (1988). *Parenting: A skills training manual* (3rd ed.). State College, PA: IDEALS.

Guerney, L. (1990). *Parenting adolescents—a supplement to parenting: A skills training program.* Silver Spring, MD: IDEALS.

Guerney, L., & Ryan, V. (2013). *Group filial therapy.* Philadelphia, PA: Jessica Kingsley.

Hughes, D., & Baylin, J. (2012). *Brain-based parenting: The neuroscience of caregiving for healthy attachment.* New York, NY: W. W. Norton.

Kraft, A., & Landreth, G. (1998). *Parents as therapeutic partners: Listening to your child's play.* Muncie, IN: Jason Aronson.

Landreth, G. (2012). *Play therapy: The art of the relationship,* 3rd ed. New York, NY: Routledge.

Nelson, J. (1996). *Positive discipline.* New York, NY: Ballantine Books.

Ray, D. (2015). *A Therapist's Guide to Child Development.* New York, NY: Routledge.

Ryan, V., & Bratton, S. (2008). Child-centered/non-directive play therapy with very young children. In C. Schaefer, P. Kelly-Zion, & J. McCormick (Eds.), *Play therapy with very young children* (pp. 25–66). New York, NY: Rowman & Littlefield.

Siegel, D. J. (2012). *Hand model of brain.* Retrieved from www.youtube.com/watch?v=gm9CIJ74Oxw

Siegel, D. J., & Bryson, T. P. (2011). *The whole-brain child.* New York, NY: Delacorte Press.

Siegel, D. J., & Bryson, T. P. (2014). *No-drama discipline: The whole-brain way to calm the chaos and nurture your child's developing mind.* New York, NY: Bantam Books.

Siegel, D. J., & Hartzell, M. (2003). *Parenting from the inside out.* New York, NY: Penguin Putnam, Inc.

Sunderland, M. (2006). *The science of parenting.* New York, NY: DK Publishing.

VanFleet, R. (1994). *Filial therapy: Strengthening parent-child relationships through play.* Sarasota, FL: Professional Resources.

VanFleet, R. (2000). *A parent's handbook of filial play therapy.* Boiling Springs, PA: Play Therapy Press.

VanFleet, R., & Guerney, L. (2003). *Casebook of filial therapy.* Boiling Springs, PA: Play Therapy Press.

Supplemental Children's Literature That Can Be Used in CPRT Training

Hausman, B., & Fellman, S. (1999). *A to Z: Do you ever feel like me?* New York, NY: Dutton Children's Books.

Manning-Ramirez, L., & Salcines, M. (2001). *Playtime for Molly.* McAllen, TX: Marlin Books.

McBratney, S. (1994). *Guess how much I love you.* Cambridge, MA: Candlewick Press.

Melmed, L. (1993). *I love you as much. . ..* New York, NY: Lothrop, Lee & Shepard Books.

Munsch, R. (1986). *Love you forever.* Willowdale, Ontario, Canada: Firefly Books. ***Authors strongly recommend this book for parents.***

Supplemental Resources for Inspirational Poems/Stories about Parenting and Children

Canfield, J., & Hansen, M. (1993). *Chicken soup for the soul.* Deerfield Beach, FL: Health Communications. *Contains many poems and stories relevant to parenting.*

Rogers, F. (2003). *The world according to Mister Rogers: Important things to remember.* New York, NY: Hyperion.

Rogers, F. (2005). *Life's journey according to Mister Rogers: Things to remember along the way.* New York, NY: Hyperion.

Supplemental Resources for Feelings Lists/Charts

Boulden Publishing. www.bouldenpublishing.com. *"Children's Poster" (of feelings), and "Feelings & Faces" products, are available for purchase.*

Self Esteem Shop. www.selfesteemshop.com *"Feelings" poster and additional resources are available in Spanish and English.*

Additional Resources for Professional Development

Note: The Center for Play Therapy houses all publications on CPRT/filial therapy, including all research. To view online, go to www.cpt.unt.edu/playlit

Bratton, S., Ceballos, P., Landreth, G., & Costas, M. (2011). Child parent relationship therapy (CPRT) with parents of sexually-abused children. In P. Goodyear-Brown (Ed.), *Handbook of child sexual abuse: Prevention, assessment, and treatment* (pp. 321–339). New York, NY: John Wiley.

Bratton, S., & Crane, J. (2003). Filial/family play therapy with single parents. In R. VanFleet & L. Guerney (Eds.), *Casebook of filial therapy.* Boiling Springs, PA: Play Therapy Press.

Bratton, S., Holt, K., & Ceballos, P. (2011). An integrative humanistic play therapy approach to treating adopted children with a history of attachment disruptions. In A. Drewes, S. Bratton, & C. Schaefer (Eds.), *Integrative play therapy* (pp. 341–370). New York, NY: John Wiley.

Bratton, S., Landreth, G., & Lin, Y. (2010). Child parent relationship therapy (CPRT): A review of controlled-outcome research. In J. Baggerly, D. Ray, & S. Bratton (Eds.), *Child-centered play therapy research: The evidence-base for effective practice*. New York, NY: John Wiley.

Brazelton, T., & Cramer, B. (1991). *The earliest relationship: Parents, infants, and the drama of early attachment*. New York, NY: Perseus Books.

Carnes-Holt, K., & Bratton, S. C. (2014). The efficacy of child parent relationship therapy for adopted children with attachment disruptions. *Journal for Counseling and Development*, *92*, 328–337.

Cozolino, L. (2014). *The neuroscience of psychotherapy: Healing the social brain*. New York, NY: W. W. Norton & Company. Inc.

Fuchs, N. (1957). Play therapy at home. *Merrill-Palmer Quarterly*, *3*, 87–95.

Greenspan, S., & Greenspan, N. (1985). *First feelings: Milestones in the emotional development of your baby and child*. New York, NY: Penguin Books.

Guerney, B., Guerney, L., & Andronico, M. (1966). Filial therapy. *Yale Scientific Magazine*, *40*, 6–14.

Guerney, L. (1976). Filial therapy program. In D. H. Olson (Ed.), *Treating relationships* (pp. 67–91). Lake Mills, IA: Graphic Publishing.

Guerney, L. (1987). *The parenting skills program: Leader's manual*. State College, PA: IDEALS.

Guerney, L. (1988). *Parenting: A skills training manual* (3rd ed.). State College, PA: IDEALS.

Guerney, L. (2000). Filial therapy into the 21st century. *International Journal of Play Therapy*, *9*(2), 1–17.

Guerney, L., & Guerney, B. (1989). Child relationship enhancement: Family therapy and parent education. Special issue: Person-centered approaches with families. *Person Centered Review*, *4*(3), 344–357.

Moustakas, C. (1959). The therapeutic approach of parents. In *Psychotherapy with children: The living relationship* (pp. 271–277). New York, NY: Harper & Row.

Opiola, K., & Bratton, S. (2018). The efficacy of child parent relationship therapy for adopted children with attachment disruptions. *Journal for Counseling and Development*, *96*(4), 155–166.

Ortwein, M. C. (1997). *Mastering the magic of play: A training manual for parents in filial therapy*. Silver Spacing, MD: Ideals.

Perry, B. D., & Szalavitz, M. (2006). *The boy who was raised as a dog and other stories from a child psychiatrist's notebook: What traumatized children can teach us about loss, love, and healing*. New York, NY: Basic Books.

Ryan, V. (2007). Filial therapy: Helping children and new carers to form secure attachment relationships. *British Journal of Social Work*, *37*(4), 643–657. doi:10.1093/bjsw/bch331

Additional Resources for Parents

(Therapist should be familiar with all books recommended to parents.)

Axline, V. (1964/1986). *Dibs in search of self*. New York, NY: Ballantine Books.

Bailey, B. (2000). *I love you rituals*. New York, NY: HarperCollins.

Blackard, S. (2005). *"SAY WHAT YOU SEE" for parents and teachers*. Retrieved from www.languageof-listening.com

Brazelton, T. B., & Greenspan, S. I. (2000). *The irreducible needs of children*. Cambridge, MA: Perseus.

Campbell, R. (1992). *How to really love your child*. Colorado Springs, CO: Chariot Victor.

Campbell, R. (2000). *Relational parenting*. Chicago: Moody Press.

Faber, A., & Mazlish, E. (1990). *Liberated parents/Liberated children*. New York, NY: Avon Books.

Faber, A., & Mazlish, E. (1998). *Siblings without rivalry: How to help your children live together so you can live too*. New York, NY: Avon.

Faber, A., & Mazlish, E. (2002). *How to talk so kids will listen & listen so kids will talk*. New York, NY: Harper Collins.

Faber, J., & King, J. (2017). *How to talk so little kids will listen*. New York, NY: Avon.

Ginott, H. (2003). *Between parent and child*. New York, NY: Avon Books.

Greenspan, S., & Greenspan, N. (1985). *First feelings milestones in the emotional development of your baby and child*. New York, NY: Penguin Books.

Illg, F. L., Ames, L. B. A., & Baker, S. M. (1981). *Child behavior: Specific advice on problems of child behavior*. New York, NY: Barnes & Noble.

Kellam, T. (2008). *The Parent Survival Guide*. New York, NY: Routledge.

Nelson, J. (1996). *Positive discipline*. New York, NY: Ballantine Books.

Schaefer, C. E., & Digeronimo, T. F. (2000). *Ages and Stages: A parent's guide to normal childhood development*. New York, NY: John Wiley & Sons.

Siegel, D. J. (2012). *Hand model of brain*. Retrieved from www.youtube.com/watch?v=gm9CIJ74Oxw

Siegel, D. J., & Bryson, T. P. (2011). *The whole-brain child*. New York, NY: Delacorte Press.

Siegel, D. J., & Bryson, T. P. (2014). *No-drama discipline: The whole-brain way to calm the chaos and nurture your child's developing mind*. New York, NY: Bantam Books.

Siegel, D. J., & Hartzell, M. (2003). *Parenting from the inside out*. New York, NY: Penguin Putnam, Inc.

Sunderland, M. (2006). *The science of parenting*. New York, NY: DK Publishing.

ADDITIONAL RESOURCES FOR CHILDREN

Selected Relationship-Oriented Children's Books

(Many of these books are particularly relevant for adoptive/foster families)

The Way I Feel by Janan Cain

I Love You Stinky Face by Lisa Mccourt

Little Raccoon's Big Questions by Miraim Schlein

You Are All My Favorites by Sam McBratney

Guess How Much I Love You by Sam McBratney

Rosie's Family by Lori Rosove

We Belong Together by Todd Parr

A Mother for Choco by Keisko Kasza

You Are My I Love You by Maryann Cusimano

I Love You All Day Long by Fancesca Rusackas and Priscilla Burris

I Love You as Much by Laura Krauss Melmed

No Matter What by Debi Gliori

The Runaway Bunny by Margaret Wise Brown

Little Flower: A Journey of Caring by Laura McAndrew

We Adopted You, Benjamin Koo by Linda Walvoord Girard

A To Z: Do You Ever Feel Like Me? by Bonnie Hausman and Sandi Fellman

Don't Forget I Love You by Miriam Moss

Not a Box by Kate Klise (helps parent understand imaginative play)

Love You Forever by Robert Munsch

All the Colors of the Earth by Sheila Hamanaka

I Like Myself! by Karen Beaumont

Heart in the Pocket by Laurence Bourguingnon

On My Mother's Lap by Ann Herbert Scott

The Invisible String by Patrice Karse

Where's My Darling Daughter by Mij Kelly and Katherine McEwen

I Love You with All My Heart by Noris Kern

Porcupette Find a Family by Vanita Oeschlanger

It's Okay to Be Different by Todd Parr

The Kissing Hand by Audrey Penn

I'll Never Let You Go by Haute

The Dot by Peter Reynolds

A Tango Makes Three by Justin Peterson and Peter Parnell

I'm Adopted by Sheila Rotner and Sheila Kelly

Loon Summer by Barbara Santucci and Andrea Shine

In Daddy's Arms I Am Tall: African Americans Celebrating Fathers by Javaka Steptoe

The Heart and a Bottle by Oliver Jeffers

I Wish You More by Amy Krouse

You Are Special by Max Lucado

Two Hands to Love You by Diane Adams

I Love You So Much by Carl Norac

The Little Engine That Could by Watty Piper

You Are the Best Medicine by Julie Clark

The Huge Bag of Worries by Virginia Ironside

Never Ever by Jo Empson

I Love You Forever and Always by Margaret Brown

I Believe in You by Marianne Richmond

Mommy's Best Kisses by Margaret Anastas

I Love You Always and Forever by Johnathan Emmett

My Beautiful Child by Lisa Desimini

MEASUREMENTS USED IN CPRT AND FILIAL THERAPY RESEARCH

Published Instruments

The following published instruments are included because they have been used to measure CPRT therapy effectiveness. Examples of published instruments that have been used to examine changes in parental behavior as a result of filial training include the Parenting Stress Index (PSI) and the Family Environment Scale (FES). Changes in children as a result of filial training have been quantified through the use of measurements such as the Child Behavior Checklist (CBCL) and the Joseph Preschool and Primary Self-Concept Scale (JPPSCS).

Abidin, R. (2012). *Parenting stress index*. Charlottesville, VA: Pediatric Psychology Press. (The PSI can be ordered from Psychological Assessment Resources at 1-800-331-8378 or via e-mail at www.parinc.com or www.custserv@parinc.com.)

Achenbach, T. M., & Edlebrock, C. S. (2010). *Manual for the child behavior checklist and revised behavioral profile*. Burlington, VT: University of Vermont. (The CBC is available for purchase at www.aseba.org.)

Moos, R., & Moos, B. (1994). *Family environment scale manual: Development, applications, research* (3rd ed.). Palo Alto, CA: Consulting Psychologist (The FES is available for purchase at www.mindgarden.com/products/fescs.htm.)

Unpublished Instruments

The Measurement of Empathy in Adult-Child Interaction (MEACI), the Porter Parental Acceptance Scale (PPAS), and the Filial Problem Checklist (FPC) have been used frequently in filial therapy research to assess child behavior problems and to more specifically measure parent (and teacher) skills and attitudes consistent with the goals of filial therapy. **With the permission of their authors, these instruments, along with administration and scoring directions, are included in Appendix F on the accompanying Companion Website at www.routledge.com/cw/bratton** to facilitate ease of reproduction. We gratefully acknowledge Dr. Louise Guerney and Dr. Blaine Porter for allowing us to include these instruments to facilitate their use by CPRT therapy researchers.

Measurement of Empathy in Adult-Child Interactions Scale (MEACI)

The MEACI measures the ability of parents or teachers to demonstrate empathic behaviors in adult-child play sessions. The MEACI has its origins in the work of Guerney, Stover, and DeMeritt's (1968) untitled assessment that measured mothers' empathy in mother-child interactions during spontaneous play with their children. Stover, Guerney, and O'Connell (1971) revised the scale and established acceptable reliability and validity scores. Bratton et al. (1993) developed the current MEACI rating form (included below) from information obtained from Stover et al. (1971) and personal communication with Louise Guerney (April 12, 1992). Specifically, the MEACI examines three major aspects of empathic behaviors: communication of acceptance, allowing the child self-direction, and involvement with the child. Empathic behaviors are rated at 3-minute intervals during the observed parent-child play sessions.

Porter Parental Acceptance Scale (PPAS)

The PPAS was originally developed by Dr. Blaine Porter in 1954 and revised by the author in 2005 (personal communication, December, 2005). The PPAS measures parental acceptance of child, a core element in the communication of empathy and a fundamental condition needed to facilitate a child's development of positive self-worth (Bratton & Landreth, 1995). Specifically, the four subscales of the PPAS measure respect for the child's feelings and the child's right to express them, appreciation of the child's uniqueness, recognition of the child's need for autonomy and independence, and a parent's experience of unconditional love for a child.

Filial Problem Checklist (FPC)

The FPC was developed at the Individual and Family Consultation Center, Pennsylvania State University, in 1974 by Peter Horner MS to measure the effectiveness of filial therapy in reducing problematic behaviors. The FPC is a parent self-report instrument that contains 108 problematic child behaviors that parents rate to indicate the severity of the problem. A total score is obtained and used pre-treatment and post-treatment to compare parents' perception of change in their child's behavior.

References

Bratton, S., & Landreth, G. (1995). Filial therapy with single parents: Effects on parental acceptance, empathy, and stress. *International Journal of Play Therapy*, *4*(1), 61–88.

Bratton, S., Landreth, G., & Homeyer, L. (1993). An intensive three-day play therapy supervision/training model. *International Journal of Play Therapy*, *2*(2), 61–79.

Guerney, B., Stover, L., & DeMeritt, S. (1968). A measurement of empathy for parent-child interaction. *Journal of Genetic Psychology*, *112*, 49–55.

Stover, L. Guerney, B., & O'Connell, M. (1971). Measurements of acceptance, allowing self-direction, involvement, and empathy in adult-child interaction. *Journal of Psychology*, *77*, 261–269.

APPENDICES

Using the Appendices

Appendix A includes helpful organizational and practical materials for CPRT training. These materials are prepared for ease of reprinting for each new group and include (a) Parent Information Form to complete prior to Session 1 and to note important information about group participants. This form should be brought to every session; therefore we suggest inserting it in the front of the *Therapist Protocol;* (b) the *Materials Checklist* for Sessions 1–10 to help therapists know what to bring to each session; the therapist is advised to bring a few extras of all printed materials that parents will need for each session, in the likely case a parent forgets the *Parent Notebook*; (c) CPRT *Progress Notes* to document the clinical progress of individual group members throughout Sessions 1–10; and the (d) *Therapist Skills Checklist* for the novice CPRT therapist or student intern for supervision purposes and to self-assess important CPRT skills. This appendix also contains items for parents that are to be handed out separately from the *Parent Notebook* materials, including *Homemade Playdough and Paint Recipes, Special Playtime Appointment Cards, "Do Not Disturb" Template*, and *Certificates of Completion*.

Appendix B contains the *Study Guide* and is designed for the beginning CPRT therapist to review *prior to* each CPRT training session. It is not intended for use *during* the CPRT sessions. The *Study Guide* is an expanded version of the *Therapist Protocol* and is designed to provide a more in-depth explanation of content. This section begins with "*Helpful Hints for Conducting CPRT*" followed by the expanded Treatment Outlines for each session. Embedded within each Treatment Outline are shaded text boxes with additional information and examples for each training concept or activity to aid you in preparing for each session. The material in the shaded text boxes is not meant to be presented in full or memorized. In several cases, the authors have shared personal parenting experiences to illustrate a point, but it is important to use your own stories and metaphors, making teaching points in a way that feels comfortable and congruent. If you are not a parent and have little personal experience with children, do not try to pretend that you do. You can draw on your professional experience as a play therapist, teacher, and so forth, or share stories of friends' or relatives' experiences with children. For the experienced CPRT therapist, the *Study Guide* can serve as a brief review.

We suggest that therapists have the *Therapist Protocol* at hand when reviewing the *Study Guide* in preparation for each session, making any additional notes directly on the Treatment Outline for that session. **Never use the *Study Guide* during CPRT sessions**; training should not be scripted. The CPRT curriculum is designed to be used by experienced play therapists with prior training, experience, and certification in both Child-Centered Play Therapy and CPRT, as well as training and experience in facilitating group therapy. This training and experience base is necessary in order to facilitate a lively, spontaneous, and interactive group training process. Reading from the *Study Guide* would interfere with this process and impede the development of a therapeutic connection between the parents and therapist. The therapist should become familiar enough with the material in the *Study Guide* to deliver the training in his or her own unique way of engaging parents in the treatment process. As noted earlier, it is expected that the therapist will exercise clinical judgment in using these materials in order to best meet the specific needs of a particular group of parents. Note: It is also necessary to refer to the *Materials Checklist* (see Appendix A on the Companion Website) as you prepare for each training session.

Appendix C includes a poster format of the most frequently used handout, *Play Session Dos and Don'ts*, formatted so that the therapist can print it out on three colored sheets of 8½″ × 11″ paper, tape it together, and laminate it as a poster to provide a handy visual for referencing these important skills during Sessions 3–10.

Appendix D includes supplemental parent handouts and worksheets with therapist versions containing example answers. The supplemental handouts provide opportunities for additional practice of CPRT skills and are used at the discretion of the therapist's assessment of the parents' needs. The session numbers on each worksheet corresponds to when that particular skill is generally introduced or practiced. Worksheets include *Feelings Response Practice* for Session 2, *Choice Giving 101* for Session 6, *Esteem-Building Responses* for Session 7, *Encouragement vs. Praise* for Session 8, and *Advanced Limit Setting: Giving Choices as Consequences for Noncompliance* for Session 9. There is also a handout on *Structured Doll Play*. References to these optional worksheets are included in the *Study Guide* for the sessions in which we recommend their use; however, they may be used flexibly, depending on the needs of a particular group of parents. Although these supplemental worksheets are provided as additional practice for CPRT skills that a particular group of parents may be struggling to implement, the therapist is cautioned to avoid overwhelming parents with too much information or homework. Again, it is expected that the therapist will exercise clinical judgment in determining when and if to use supplemental materials.

Appendix E includes information for successful marketing of CPRT to parents. Sample flyers and brochure are included. These materials may be electronically adapted for therapist use. Note: The acronym C-P-R Training is used on all marketing materials for parents as well as materials that they receive in their parent notebooks.

Appendix F includes three unpublished assessments that have been used for research in CPRT and filial therapy: *Porter Parental Acceptance Scale* (PPAS), *Filial Problems Checklist* (FPC), and *Measurement of Empathy in Adult-Child Interaction* (MEACI). All three measures are designed to be administered pre and post treatment. The PPAS and FPC are self-report instruments administered to parents; the PPAS measures the parents' attitude of acceptance toward the child of focus, while the FPC measures the parents' perception of the child of focus's behavior. The MEACI is a direct observational measure of parental empathy that requires pre and post video-recording of parents (the use of this instrument requires substantial training and inter-rater reliability). Instruments and scoring are included in separate files for ease of printing. We gratefully acknowledge Dr. Louise Guerney and Dr. Blaine Porter for generously allowing us to include these materials for use by CPRT therapists.

Appendices Content

Note: The appendices listed below are found in the accompanying Companion Website at www.routledge.com/cw/bratton.

Appendix A: Required and Recommended Materials

- Parent Information Form (For Therapist—Session 1)
- Materials Checklist (For Therapist—1–10)
- CPRT Progress Notes for Sessions 1–10, Form A and B
- CPRT—Therapist Skill Checklists—Supervision Form and Research Integrity Form
- Homemade Play-Doh and Paint Recipes for Toddlers
- Template for "Do Not Disturb" sign
- Appointment Cards for Parents—Young Child (Sessions 3 and 10)
- Appointment Cards for Parents—Older Child (Sessions 3 and 10)
- Certificate of Completion for Parents (Session 10)

Appendix B: Study Guide

Appendix C: Dos and Don'ts Poster

Appendix D: Supplemental Parent Worksheets/ Handouts (and Therapist Answer Sheets)

- Feelings Response Practice Worksheet (for Parents—Session 2)
- Feelings Response Practice Answersheet (for Therapist—Session 2)
- Choice Giving Practice Worksheet (for Parents—Session 6)
- Choice Giving Practice Answersheet (for Therapist—Session 6)
- Esteem-Building Responses Worksheet (for Parents—Session 7)
- Esteem-Building Responses Answersheet (for Therapist—Session 7)
- Encouragement vs. Praise Worksheet (for Parents—Session 8)
- Encouragement vs. Praise Answersheet (for Therapist—Session 8)
- Advanced Limit Setting: Giving Choices as Consequences Worksheet (for Parents—Session 9)
- Advanced Limit Setting: Giving Choices as Consequences Answersheet (for Therapist—Session 9)
- Structured Doll Play for Parents handout

Appendix E: Marketing CPRT Training

- Sample Brochure
- Sample CPRT Flyer #1: Parenting Can Be Difficult
- Sample CPRT Flyer #2: Give Your Children What They Need Most: **YOU**
- Sample CPRT Flyer #3: Parenting Your Adopted Child Can Be Challenging

Appendix F: CPRT/Filial Therapy Assessments

Measurement of Empathy in Adult-Child Interaction (MEACI)
- Instrument
- Directions for Scoring

Porter Parental Acceptance Scale (PPAS)
- Instrument
- Directions for Scoring

Filial Problems Checklist (FPC)
- Instrument
- Directions for Scoring

CONTENTS OF COMPANION WEBSITE

Using the Companion Website

The Companion Website contains all necessary and supplemental training materials found in the six *Appendices*, a detailed *Study Guide, Marketing Materials,* and *Assessments*, as well as the five CPRT protocols provided in a format that allows for ease of reproduction and enhanced usability. Protocols include:

- **CPRT Protocol—Ages 3 to 10** and **Parent Notebook**
- **Toddler Adapted CPRT Protocol** and **Parent Notebook**
- **Preadolescent Adapted CPRT Protocol** and **Parent Notebook**
- **Adoptive Families Adapted CPRT Protocol** and **Parent Notebook**
- **Teacher/Student Adapted Protocol** and **Teacher Notebook**

Note: Permission to copy the materials is granted to the therapist for personal use in conjunction with the purchase of this training. The copyright statement should be included on all printed materials.

Companion Website

CPRT Protocol – Ages 3–10
- Therapist Protocol: Treatment Outlines and Handouts for Sessions 1–10
- Parent Notebook

CPRT-Toddler Protocol
- Therapist Protocol: Treatment Outlines and Handouts for Sessions 1–10
- Parent Notebook

CPRT-Preadolescent Protocol
- Therapist Protocol: Treatment Outlines and Handouts for Sessions 1–10
- Parent Notebook

CPRT-Adoptive Families Protocol
- Therapist Protocol: Treatment Outlines and Handouts for Sessions 1–10
- Parent Notebook

CPRT for Teachers-Students: Child-Teacher Relationship Training (CTRT) Protocol
- Therapist Protocol: Treatment Outlines and Handouts for Sessions 1–10
- Teacher Notebook

Appendix A: Required and Recommended Materials

- Parent Information Form (For Therapist—Session 1)
- Materials Checklist (For Therapist—1–10)
- CPRT Progress Notes for Sessions 1–10, Form A and B
- CPRT—Therapist Skill Checklist s—Supervision Form and Research Integrity Form
- Homemade Play-Doh and Paint Recipes for Toddlers
- Template for "Do Not Disturb" sign
- Appointment Cards for Parents—Young Child (Sessions 3 and 10)
- Appointment Cards for Parents—Older Child (Sessions 3 and 10)
- Certificate of Completion for Parents (Session 10)

Appendix B: Study Guide

Appendix C: Dos and Don'ts Poster

Appendix D: Supplemental Parent Handouts/Worksheets (and Therapist Answer Sheets)

- Feelings Response Practice Worksheet (for Parents—Session 2)
- Feelings Response Practice Answersheet (for Therapist—Session 2)
- Choice Giving Practice Worksheet (for Parents—Session 6)
- Choice Giving Practice Answersheet (for Therapist—Session 6)
- Esteem-Building Responses Worksheet (for Parents—Session 7)
- Esteem-Building Responses Answersheet (for Therapist—Session 7)
- Encouragement vs. Praise Worksheet (for Parents—Session 8)
- Encouragement vs. Praise Answersheet (for Therapist—Session 8)
- Advanced Limit Setting: Giving Choices as Consequences Worksheet (for Parents—Session 9)
- Advanced Limit Setting: Giving Choices as Consequences Answersheet (for Therapist—Session 9)
- Structured Doll Play for Parents handout

Appendix E: Marketing CPRT Training

- Sample Brochures and Flyers

Appendix F: Assessments

Measurement of Empathy in Adult-Child Interaction (MEACI)
- Instrument
- Directions for Scoring

Porter Parental Acceptance Scale (PPAS)
- Instrument
- Directions for Scoring

Filial Problems Checklist (FPC)
- Instrument
- Directions for Scoring